Lincolnshire
COUNTY COUNCIL

discover libraries

This book should be returned on or before the last date shown below.

To renew or order library books please telephone 01522 782010
or visit www.lincolnshire.gov.uk

You will require a Personal Identification Number.
Ask any member of staff for this.

D1355505

04873174

LANDER'S WAR
1914-1919

The War Diaries of Lt Charles Herbert Lander
10th Battalion, Royal Warwickshire Regiment

MENIN HOUSE

Menin House
an imprint of Tommies Guides
Military Booksellers & Publishers

Menin House
13 Hunloke Avenue
Eastbourne
East Sussex
BN22 8UL

www.tommiesguides.co.uk

First published in Great Britain by Menin House Publishers 2010

© 2010 Charles Lander, Michael Harrison (ed)

A catalogue record for this book
is available from the British Library

ISBN 978-0-9563-4264-5

Cover design by Tommies Guides
Typeset by Tommies Guides
Printed and bound in Great Britain by CPI Antony Rowe,
Chippenham and Eastbourne

Contents

Acknowledgements

The publisher wishes to thank the following for their help and advice in the preparation of this work. Professor Richard Holmes, Peter Hart of the Imperial War Museum and members of The Guild of Battlefield Guides for their support in enabling this book to be pubished.

Publisher's Note

This narrative is based on original notes and diary entries and as such has been edited to interpret the hand of Charles Lander in the right spirit – keeping to the jotting style but tidying up the punctuation from ways which are not used in that manner nowadays and were therefore difficult to follow at times.

The use of abbreviated terminology and titles has been made consistent and is used throughout the work to keep with the familiar style the author was writing these memoirs up in during the 1930's. The reader will find a useful glossary at the rear of the book for any unfamiliar terms.

Some assumptions have been made in compiling this work, namely the use of "x" in relating to distances. It was typical at the time to refer to distances in paces or an approximate yard so 250x relates to 250 yards.

All map references relate to the 1,000 yard grid system for WW1 British Army trench maps. Whilst often abbreviated in the diary entry, for the experienced reader of maps, the exact location can be found in conjunction with the context in which it is written. For those wishing to find more information on trench maps we recommend the Western Front Association, the National Archives at Kew, the Imperial War Museum or the National Army Museum.

For a useful description on how to read trench maps please visit The Long, Long Trail on the Internet; http://www.1914-1918.net/trench_maps.htm

Foreword
Professor Richard Holmes

Howover much I mean to write my last word about the First World War I am drawn back to it despite myself. Somehow there is no escaping this conflict that stands like a barrier between present and past, a division made all the starker by the death, in 2009, of the last fighting Tommy. What was, for so much of my life, a matter of reminiscence is now the business of history. It is important to remember that, while the Second World War was a much bigger global event, for Britain alone the First World War was more damaging in terms of the casualties it caused and more comprehensive for the men it swept into uniform. It was also one of those rare occasions on which the British army confronted, in a war's main theatre, the greatest strength of a major continental opponent, and the British experience is comprehensible only in terms of a tiny peacetime army expanding to become the biggest that this nation has ever put into the field.

Charles Lander's diary seems to have been maintained during the war, and was, as he tells us, written up in the form that we now see it nearly twenty years after the events it describes. Although it is impossible to be sure how much reworking this involved, the present version is redolent of the mood of the moment. In so many respects Lander is a typical man of his age and class, a former grammar school boy who had just finished attending Birmingham University Officers' Training Corps camp when war broke out. Although, like so many of his O.T.C. comrades, he held the certificates that should have enabled him to obtain a commission. in the heady mood of August 1914, with so many young men using whatever influence they could to become officers, the process suddenly seemed ridiculously hard, and so he joined a Territorial battalion, 2/6th Royal Warwicks, as a private soldier. He found himself serving alongside many of his old schoolmates in a well-motivated battalion in which crime was almost unknown, and was a corporal in a fortnight and a sergeant by the war's first Christmas.

Commissioned in February 1915, he provided himself with the recommended kit ('quite a lot of it useless for an officer in war time'), did a short officer-training course at Cambridge and was then posted to 10th Royal Warwickshire Regiment, a 'New Army' (wartime raised) battalion that was then at Tidworth in Hampshire, at full strength and ready to go abroad as part of 57th Brigade in 19th (Western) Division. This division was to serve continuously on the Western Front from mid-1916 until the end of the war, taking part in the battle of the Somme in 1916, though providentially it was in reserve on the first day, and the battles of Messines Ridge and Passchendaele in 1917.

In 1918 it first bore the brunt of the German March offensive and was then shifted to Flanders in time to catch the next phase of the attack, the Battle of the Lys, in April. Out of the line to retrain in the summer of 1918, 19th Division returned to fight in the last battles of the Hundred Days, though it had been pulled back into reserve just before the war ended. In all it suffered just over 39,000 casualties, turning over more than twice its establishment strength.

Although he sometimes served in brigade headquarters, Charles Lander's main preoccupation was with the introspective world of his battalion. He formed close friends, and Lieutenant F. P. Smith who, like him, was to survive the war, was his best man when he married in 1918. Regimental Sergeant Major Pratt, killed in 1917, was 'a dear good natured soul and loved by everybody. He was badly hit in the side near Klein Zillebeke and refused aid from the stretcher bearers, walking all the way back to the dressing station near the Spoil Bank where he collapsed and died.' Commanding officers were a mixed bunch. His first was a 'great friend to all,' but he could not see why a subsequent commanding officer was awarded the DSO 'and I was with him at headquarters all the time.' Majors were often uninspiring. One was 'a vile type of old army major', another introduced riding lessons as a means of 'bullying wretched officers', and two more, 'thoroughly inefficient,' were sent home before they could get men killed. In an echo of Siegfried Sassoon's 'scarlet majors at the base', the depot battalion at Parkhurst on the Isle of Wight seemed 'full of dugout majors, the type who went sick when there was anything doing, and who drank and played bridge all day'. One of his company commanders was basically a decent man but treated his malaria with two bottles of whisky and ample quinine each day. His subalterns unwisely tried to protect him by holding him on his bed when he had the DTs, but eventually he lost his commission. Formed up before the officers, he was told that 'the King had no further need of his services', and was sent off to the Provost Marshal under escort.

Lander saw a good deal of front-line service. His baptism of fire, in early July just north of the Arras-Bapaume road on the Somme, was unsettling, for he found his company was dug in amidst the debris of earlier attacks and, slipping in the mud he reached out to steady himself and found that he had grabbed the head of a dead British soldier. Sent into Mametz Wood to reconnoitre for his battalion's advance he found the place liberally strewn with the dead of both sides, and admitted that the flies were 'having a really good summer'.

Because he often includes map references we can sometimes trace his movements very accurately, and his account of moving up the road from Flatiron Copse into Bazentin le Petit is especially chilling, for he walked in past 'smouldering masses of our own dead and dying', because the flash of German high-explosive shells had set fire to uniforms.

He saw how capricious death could be. His commanding officer on the Somme, desperate to relieve himself, went up from his dugout into the trench above just as a shell arrived. 'I could see the colonel's bare back,' he wrote, 'with a small hole that leaked blood, and his stomach was lying open and mixed up with the fallen earth.' Later, he was cooped up under heavy bombardment with an officer with shell-shock, when another officer was 'dragged in badly hit in the back, his kidneys were all exposed and we couldn't find a dressing big enough to cover the hole, so we did the best we could and gave him morphine to keep him quiet; we got him away later and he survived'. Lander was always prepared to do his bit but was never sorry to be wounded. He was hit in the hand by shrapnel as the CO was looking for somebody to lead a forlorn hope on the Somme, a fortunate escape, and in May 1918 he was wounded in hand and leg: 'Oh! Joy – a Blighty one and so convenient too; to get a couple of miles from the line was all we prayed for'.

Like so many front-line soldiers Lander was ambivalent about the Germans. News of the sinking of the *Lusitania*, received while the battalion was still in Tidworth 'made us all very keen to get out and have a go at them'. On the Somme, however, he saw German prisoners working in a Casualty Clearing Station: 'they were doing good work and returning time after time to the battlefield in search of stretcher cases. Other German wounded were cheerfully giving a hand and smoking with our fellows as though they had always been the best of pals'. Not long afterwards he met some Germans in an Advanced Dressing Station: 'They seemed a bit timid and our wounded were giving them cigarettes, tea and chocolate and doing their best to make them feel at home. Truly a most extraordinary spirit of comradeship after all the bloody encounters of the past five months'. German prisoners taken on Messines Ridge – 'the usual smug faced lot' – seemed relieved to be out of it, but one 'big bug,' a regimental commander, demanded an officer escort. Instead, he was sent off in the charge of the scruffiest private in the battalion who promptly stole his badges and consigned him to the other ranks' prisoner-of-war cage.

When he is critical of the high command his judgements seem fair. He thought that the real reason for failure on 1 July 1916 was inadequate artillery preparation, and his own brigade's inability to take Grandcourt at the year's end reflected the high command's failure to understand the ground and weather conditions: 'Even had we been successful it would have meant spending winter in low lying ground instead of remaining on the high ground which we already held'. His own division was to blame in not allowing any reconnaissance, and the attacking units, familiar with their ground, were moved about at the last moment. When his battalion was out of the line in early August 1916 – 'three perfect days of ease and good living' – the colonel allowed men to parade in shirts and shorts 'but some Johnny on the staff thought this dress unbecoming to soldiers of HM the King so we had to go back into full kit'. In contrast, he was full of praise for (General) Plumers's plan for Messines Ridge, which included 'great concentration of infantry and arrangements for a slow methodical advance under a perfect barrage', as well as the shattering effect of the mines fired beneath German positions and the liberal distribution of accurate maps.

He has a good deal to say about those hardy perennials, food and accommodation. When the division came out of the line in November 1917 'there was little peace, even the divisional band could not raise any enthusiasm. Everyone was lousy and spent most of their time scraping the fat louse from the backs of their shirts and from the seams of their uniforms... The huts were very filthy and overcrowded, and the stink [...] will never be forgotten'. Coming home on leave in late 1917 he found an excellent meal on the train that took him from Dover to London: 'a good honest steak with chips and beer. I never before appreciated a meal or life so much as I did that afternoon'.

There are some timeless judgements. When he was commanding a scratch company in April 1918 he was worried because 'the men were half asleep and grousing very little which was a bad sign; in fact they seemed lifeless; few knew their officers and we knew less of the men; it was fortunate that there still survived a few old sweats, the type who never die; they did their best to cheer things up.'

Soldiers hated the working parties that were so often a feature of life out of the line, and in July 1917 resented time spent collecting 'old arms, ammunition, shell cases, clothing etc from captured ground, for 'they knew that munition workers at home that were making anything from £10 to £20 a week and threatening all the time to strike for more...' His battalion lost 'three of its finest officers [...] fooling about at night in no man's land', and believed that 'the whisky bottle had a lot to do with it.' What we now call 'blue on blue' was all too frequent, with patrols missing their way in the dark or men failing to respond to the challenge of sentries.

Like so many survivors, Charles Lander had his share of luck. He was away on a course when the storm broke on 21 March 1918, and was in Britain during the last costly advance on Mons. In November 1916 he went on a reconnaissance with the assistant adjutant and the pair were sniped at: his companion went out again shortly afterwards and was shot through the head. He is refreshingly honest. He was 'not very handy with a revolver', so much so that he was reluctant even to attempt to finish off a wounded horse. When his battalion attacked on 18 November 1916 he admitted that 'I for one was in a frightful funk', and after he had been wounded in April 1918 and had to wait under gas attack in an aid post 'I prayed and cursed the Boche alternately'. This is an evocative account of an infantry officer's war, its occasional grimness illuminated by flashes of humour, an honest testimony from a generation that endured.

Richard Holmes, 2010.

Introduction
Michael Harrison, Editor

I first had the privilege of meeting Charles Lander's daughter Mary in 2007. The meeting had been arranged through a mutual friend with a view to finding a publisher for the memoirs of her father, Charles Herbert Lander, who had served and fought as an officer in the British Army during the Great War. Our meeting proved to be the first of many on the long hard road to publication. Mary is a gentle soul of the Catholic persuasion, living in her deceased parents' fabulous Edwardian house with a convent at the bottom of the huge, well kept garden.

Mary and I hit it off immediately and when she produced her father's memoir it took only a few minutes of perusal to realize that what we had was a document of the utmost importance to anyone with even the slightest interest in the Great War. There have been many old soldiers' diaries and memoirs from the Great War that have been deemed worthy of publication. Unfortunately a number of these, although of great historical value, prove to be a difficult read for the younger or casual reader as names and locations are often omitted. Not so with 'Lander's War'. Charles tells us how it was and who were the players in the great game, as they appear and all too often disappear from his pages. It is no exaggeration to say that when reading this work some families in the U.K. will discover the exact fate that befell their ancestors. Charles had no idea that his work would ever be published, so he saw no need for anonymity when working on his memoir in the year 1920. What Charles Lander has passed down to us through his daughter is a factual and most important document, detailing the life of an ordinary young man, swept up by the tide of chaos that engulfed the world and could so easily have destroyed our freedoms forever.

A family tradition relates that the Lander family originated in Loughborough and they may well have been attracted to Birmingham by the city's reputation as 'the city of a thousand trades'. Here it was said that folk walked barefoot into Birmingham and left in their own gilded coach and four. In those days the city was famous as a centre of the toy trade, this did not mean children's playthings but small, intricately made, metal objects.

The Landers would eventually set up as manufacturing jewellers at 70 Great Hampton Street, an ancient thoroughfare running North West from the city centre. Life didn't always run smoothly as is evidenced by the family history, which tells of some family members losing all their money in the wake of the collapse of the Birmingham Banking Company in 1866. By the year 1795, two brothers, George and John are known to have been living in St Paul's Square which is home to the beautiful church of that name. The church building is famous for not having an East window, instead the 'window' is painted on the inside wall behind the altar. The family had wide business interests prior to becoming manufacturing jewellers ranging from gun making, cabinet and coffin making, glass and toy making, pattern making, plating, japanning, drapery, general merchants and shoemakers.

Charles was born in 1893 when the family was living in the Handsworth district of Birmingham; he spent part of his school life at the famous Handsworth Grammar School before moving to Solihull School when the family re-located to "Estcourt" Ashleigh Road, Solihull. Solihull School ran an Officers' Training Corps unit (O.T.C.) of which Charles became a member. Further education followed at Birmingham College of Art and he also enrolled into Birmingham University O.T.C., in which, he attended a training camp when war broke out in August 1914. Here was a keen young man with a fair knowledge of military matters and good at sports, from a family that ate far better than much of the population of Britain at that time, and yet, because of his not uncommon poor physique he was deemed unfit for service.

This woeful state of affairs with the nation's well being would prove to be of grave concern to the Authorities as they strove to rapidly expand the army. It was while serving in the university O.T.C. that Charles was to make the acquaintance of one, William Joseph Slim, who was later to do well in his army career, becoming a field marshal and a viscount. Charles became a member of the unofficial "Slim's Lambs" a keen bunch who seemed to excel at their training exercises. Bill Slim as he was known, took a commission in the Royal Warwickshire Regiment as did another lad who would go on to achieve the rank of field marshal; Bernard Law Montgomery. As for Charles Lander, he had to wait until the chest measurement was reduced before he could apply as a private soldier with the 2/6th Battalion Royal Warwickshire Regiment.

Upon his commission, Charles was to serve in the 10th Battalion which was a part of 57th Brigade, 19th (Western) Division. Read on, and let Charles take you into the tumultuous world of the Great War; there are moments of comedy, low points, sheer terror and wonder as to how humans could endure, go home and live again in everyday society. Lt Charles Herbert Lander truly had the skill to pull back the curtains on the window of time; with his words, he took me to the now quiet far off fields of France and Flanders, now transformed from the most dangerous places on Earth to their former rural peace. *Are you willing to take the first step?*

Michael Harrison (editor), 2009.

1914

Birmingham Officer Training Corps (O.T.C.), 1914.
Author's collection.

There were rumours of war, but those of us who were in camp on Windmill Hill with the senior battalion of the Offficers Training Corps (O.T.C.) took little or no notice of these rumours, there had been so many the past few years, thanks to the Daily Mail. Most of us were there for the sport of the thing, though naturally we all took a keen interest in showing up well against other universities. Many of us had cert[ificate]s A and B and were really quite proficient in company drill, musketry etc., but how little of this was to be of real use to us in the Great War which was so near upon us!

Looking back it seems extraordinary how very limited was the conception of what a modern European war might develop into. It is quite understandable that gas was not mentioned as being against international law, but there was no mention of trench warfare; bombs,mortar and creeping barrage by artillery had not been thought of (it was all about superiority of infantry fire and the bayonet assault). Tanks not invented and aeroplanes which only flew in the morning and evening were apparently destined to be used only as corps or army scouts, no one had the vision to see how useful they would be for keeping contact with infantry and spotting for the guns. By August 2nd war was certain though few of us realised it.

❖

August 2nd

Camp was struck and we were all packed off home hurriedly after being asked who would take the commission in case of war being declared. I think all of us put our names down but that was all that happened; none of us got commissions through that first application. Weeks went by and papers galore were sent into O.T.C. orderly rooms applying for commissions in any unit; but still nothing happened; put in the waste paper basket or pigeon holed at the War Office; probably there now, and what had all the money been spent on the O.T.C. for, surely this was the day we had been training for? It was very annoying for us to hear that numbers of our friends who had had no military experience were getting commissions quite easily because they knew some old colonel who would nominate them for his own battalion. In desperation, many O.T.C. boys who would have made first class officers joined the ranks of new battalions then being raised, because we all knew that the war could not last more than a few months longer. A new difficulty now presented itself, myself included as although I was perfectly fit I happen to be under chest measurement (then 35 inches) and after having paid fruitless visits to Warwick had to wait until chest measure was reduced to 34 inches.

❖

October 30th – 31st

Doing no business and being thoroughly fed up and a little sensitive to the looks some men in khaki gave me I decided to try my luck at Thorpe Street where the second line territorial battalions were being raised, chest measure being reduced for these second-class troops. I had no difficulty in saying "99" – was accepted as Pte C.H. Lander 3124 2/6 Royal Warwickshire Regiment (R Wks Rgt) (number later altered to 3363), Col. Graham in command. I received my first day's pay: 1/- and ration allowance 1/9d, and went home with very mixed feelings as to what Pa would say and as to how things would turn out. I joined on Saturday morning 30th October [19]14 and did not have to report until Monday morning; little did I realise what the future was to be and never did I expect that I should not get back to business and civilian life for another 4 ½ years.

❖

November 12th – 14th

The 2/6th were a very mixed crowd, good fellows at heart most of them, but in their very mixed civilian attire they looked very doubtful company. The battalion was at first organised on the old eight company formation with four sections per company and four squadrons to a section. I was posted to "Q" Company composed of non manual workers under Capt. Wade (C.C. Wade, metal merchant) and discovered amongst the company a number of old school friends from Handsworth Grammar School, who had all joined together, so that I soon settled down and thoroughly enjoyed the new life. We were all great pals, much better than we had been at school. A little clique dined together each day at Ridgbay's Café. Three months were spent at Thorpe Street, training by day - morning and afternoon parades in Edgbaston Park, chiefly squad, section drill and musketry instruction. My previous training enabled me to get a section from the first; I did not fancy being only a private and did my best to push on and was made a full corporal at the end of the second week; being then sent to Warwick depot to be dished out with complete set of uniform (no equipment or arms) complete with two stripes, of which I was very proud really. In these newly raised battalions, the old type of army N.C.O. whose only qualification for the rank was his parrot like knowledge of the drill books - a good pair of bellows - and an infinite capacity for drinking was entirely missing and as we were mostly very keen to learn. Life for the N.C.Os. was not difficult as we all helped one another. There was very little crime; only a few drunks, the type of man who would always get drunk and then through being incapable of doing otherwise, cut parade. These were carefully dealt with and humoured by the very young officers and N.C.Os. The worst types we had amongst us were the mentally deficient who had been passed in by an inefficient medical officer too intent on getting his attestation fees, backed up by a regular orderly room N.C.O. who no doubt got his 1/- per head also.

Towards the end of November the company commander sent for me to attend a lecture in the billiard room on the mysteries of the pay and mess book and from that day on I acted as company quartermaster sergeant, with extra pay 6d a day (later raised to 1/- a day when the battalion came under the new four-company organisation). These duties had to be combined with my instructor's job: no time off, which was most unfair considering that later on in the war when everybody was more efficient C.Q.Ms. did no parades. Every evening till near midnight had to be spent swatting over these wretched pay sheets; which to us young N.C.Os. were much more complicated than filling up income tax returns of the present day. In addition there were lodging allowance forms to make out for men living at home and the red tape of the Warwick pay office would not allow ditto. ditto etc, and results looked like school compositions. I had one of these returned which resulted in my first ticking off by the company commander but he knew no more than I did and I was let off with a caution as it was Christmas, said he, suppressing a smile.

─────── ❖ ───────

December 18th

Just before Christmas I was promoted full sergeant and it fell to my lot to be sergeant of the guard on Christmas Eve, my first guard at the drill hall, Thorpe Street. We had no arms of course, the sentry on the gate just carrying a thick stick and we had no lock up for the prisoners; prisoners and guard mucking in together in the guard room. Not a very happy position for the sergeant of the guard if prisoners adopted a fighting attitude and many of them did when in liquor; tactfully to humour them was my only hope at the same time keeping them away from the door in case they decided to bolt. One of our best sergeants was reduced to the ranks for allowing a prisoner to escape. Nobby Pincher was the unfortunate sergeant, and we all protested (very unmilitary) but a private he remained for a long time. Christmas passed and January, and again being sergeant of the guard, about midnight on Feb 1st, I was called by the sentry on the gate. On going to investigate discovered that the telephone in the C.O.'s office kept ringing. Answering the call I took down my first real military signal message plentifully punctuated with AAA which in those days was Greek to me. The message was to the effect that the battalion would move on Feb 4th to billet in Northampton (H.Q. Eastern Command). This was real news and I passed on the message to Col. Graham at his private address.

For me the most enjoyable parades while in B'ham had been the weekly wash at Kent Street Baths – bathing parade of all shapes and sizes. Feb 4th came and we moved in the evening; entrained at New Street Station; marching en route from the barracks through a great throng of civilians cheering and weeping; many seemed to think we were going away for the last time, though we were still in our civvy clothes except the N.C.Os. and officers; the battalion was at full strength. Arriving at Northampton late in the evening we were marched to Far Cotton where we were to be billeted for some months to come. Sgt Lansley and myself were rather lucky in getting fixed up with a very good billet at No. 110, Oxford Street, with a Mr and Mrs Grimley: dear old people who did all they could to make us comfortable in their humble home. Mr Grimley was a signalman on the L.N.W.R., a strong trade unionist and of course a socialist and many were the arguments we had over politics; which almost invariably had to be left unfinished as he got rather worked up when we were only pulling his leg most of the time.

Here we drew our rations from the store each day and added a little ourselves and did very well. The old girl was a good cook and everything was clean and fanciable, which was much more than could be said for many of the billets further down the road; many were very low and unclean. All my time here was spent in training as at B'ham with the addition of early morning physical jerks. Lansley and myself slept in the same room and had to get an alarm clock to get us out in time or I'm sure we should have lost our stripes, for it was hard to get up these cold mornings and neither of us were used to early rising. We took it in turns to make an early cup of tea.

While at Northampton the battalion was issued with uniforms and rifles but no equipment till after I left. The rifles were Japanese; slightly smaller bore than the British. I believe they had higher velocity, they were quite a good job really but as the wood part was polished a pale yellow colour they looked like the rifles of toy soldiers.

While at Northampton we learnt that the battalion was in the 61st Division and that should our first line battalion be sent overseas, we should have to take their place in the defence of London down by Billericay in Essex.

We were now training in double companies; eg. sixteen platoons to each battalion – four in each Coy. The old "Q" Company having joined up with another to form "D" Company 13, 14, 15, and 16 Platoons under Capt. Wade and Capt. Lawley, and, as I was senior Sgt. and a company sgt-major is required, I was hoping to get my crown. But, owing to the fact that I was given a commission, this was not to be. Sgt Howse became C.S.M. after I left and eventually he became R.S.M. when the Battalion went to France in 1916.

❖

Birmingham Officer Training Corps (O.T.C.), 1914.
Charles Lander is kneeling front row, second from left.

"Slim's Lambs". Birmingham University O.T.C. 1914.
Charles Lander is seated in the middle. On 22nd August 1914, Slim became a second
lieutenant in the Royal Warwickshire Regiment (standing middle). Slim became
renowned for his leadership in Burma during the Second World War. In 1948 he
achieved the highest post in the British Army, Chief of the Imperial General Staff
(CIGS) and in January 1949 was promoted Field Marshal. Author's collection.

Charles Lander 1914. 2nd 6th Royal Warwickshire Regiment.
Outside his home in Ashleigh Road, Solihull. Author's Collection.

1915

Tidworth Training Camp. 1915.
Publisher's collection.

February 26th

I was sent for by the C.O. and appeared rather nervously at the orderly room as I did not know what was wrong. The adjutant saw me and congratulated me; shook hands and bid me leave for home that very night, as the instructions from the War Office were to the effect that I was to be discharged from that date; and had to report at Cambridge on 4th March for a course of instruction; in the meantime a few days leave while getting my kit together. I just had time to collect my traps from the billet and bid farewell to friend Lansley; could not find the company commander to say goodbye and hand over company rolls etc.; so wrote him a letter of explanation and apologies for my haste in clearing off so suddenly; which by the way he never bothered to answer.

The next few days spent buying kit as per printed list; quite a lot of it useless for an officer in war time; but there was no one to advise and most of us blindly followed the War Office instruction and bought the lot; the £50 grant for kit seemed such a big sum to most of us though really it was about £10 short of what we really spent.

❖

March 4th

My friend F.P. Smith was commissioned same day and by great good fortune was ordered to report to Cambridge also; and so we went on 4th March to Cambridge complete with swords looking very new officers. Arriving at Cambridge I was quartered in Pembroke College and F.P. Smith at Peterhouse. Then began the most intensive training of my whole army life. So much had to be crowded into the four weeks here, and the discipline also was excessively strict; the penalty for any misbehaviour was a report to the War Office that you were not likely to become an efficient officer: this had the desired effect always. Capt. Montieth took the outdoor parades (he was home on sick leave) and university professors the lectures on map reading, military law etc. We were kept at it till 9.30pm each evening except when we had night operations when it would probably be 2am before we got back as we invariably got lost on these stunts; and Sunday was no day of rest either. A youngster named Lowry shared quarters with me, a real Scot. A whole company of officers messed together in Hall which was always a parade. The messing was of course good but very expensive: 5/6 a day out of our pay which was then

7/6 a day, the college taking our ration allowance of 1/9 a day also. This was rather serious for many and I wondered whether I had made a mistake taking a commission as at this rate it was not possible to live on one's pay. We were examined at end of course and a report sent to our units; we were allowed a few days leave at the end of the month before reporting to our respective units for duty.

❖

April 8th

Reporting for duty at Tidworth I found that the 10th Service Battalion R Wks R was quartered in Kandahar Barracks. It was at full strength and very efficient and expecting to go overseas at any moment. The battalion had been raised and trained by Col. Bastley McCalmont C.B., a real old topper, only suffering severely from gout, which eventually deprived him of the honour of taking his beloved battalion overseas.

We were part of the 57th Infantry Brigade in the 19th Division. Brigadier was Brig.-Gen. Twyford (P... Corner as he was called by some owing to his connection in civil life with the pottery firm). There were a number of supernumerary officers of whom I was one and we were in tents as there was no room in the officers' quarters; for this I was very thankful as it meant little inconvenience and an extra 2/6 per day field allowance which after Cambridge helped my financial situation considerably.

I was posted to "B" Company as supernumerary to No.7 Platoon, the company being in command of a Capt. Owen who had the Queen's South Africa medal and was thought no end of a lad in consequence. He did not appeal to my ideals; and it was not long before I ran foul of him because I did as most others did and cut an early morning parade on a day when he turned up himself, and being what he was and me the last to join, I was up for C.O. orders next morning. What a night; I thought, the King would have no further need of my services; but fortunately in the morning he was in better humour and I pleading for another chance, did get let off and so did not have to interview the C.O. I felt much better.

There was a vile type of old army major as second in command, who always slashed and kicked his horse on parade and whose pet aversion was young subalterns. He broke one of the finest young officers in the battalion by putting in an adverse report about him for spite: it was the dirty way it was done which made one boil. The subaltern's first intimation was a note from the War Office telling him to resign his commission and there was no chance of an enquiry and no redress, it had gone too far.

While here, the battalion was doing advanced training and finally polishing up before going to France. The musketry course was fired at Bulford and a number of inspections by big-wigs were taking place. I missed most of these as I was not going out with the battalion: I had to do extra orderly officers jobs, inspection of rations and meals etc., and not forgetting to sample the canteen beer with the sergeant major, which was always done at closing time.

About this time we heard of the sinking by the Germans of the *Lusitania* which made us all very mad to get out and have a go at them. There was also about this time an outbreak of measles which caused a number of us to miss the last big field operations which lasted four days. The officers with the measles including myself were stowed away in one of the empty houses in the married quarters and we did ourselves right well in the food line, but was very boring as we were outcasts: Lts Herbert, Whitworth and Haltwood were among the measles. The measles over, meant a week's leave and while on leave the battalion moved to France, the only casualty en route being a mule which fell out of the train in France and was killed. Very careless of the transport officer; he was never allowed to forget it.

❖

July 20th

At the end of leave we were sent with other supernumerary officers to join the 13th Reserve Battalion R Wks R then in hutments on the cliffs at Swanage, Isle of Purbeck under the command of Col. Graham White. With the exception of four weeks in August spent at a course near Portsmouth, the rest of the summer was spent here; a real holiday. It was very little work; plenty of sea bathing and plenty of legs, female legs. While here I did a course of signalling under 2nd-Lt Taylor; who had been to school with me at Handsworth Grammar. This course was to have a big effect on my future duties and movements. The country round here was fine and we had plenty of time to enjoy it. The colonel was not the type who looked down on young temporary officers and was a great friend to all. My company commander was Capt. Muir, also a very decent sort.

❖

August

The general course of instruction I was sent to at Portsmouth was a very good one; except that the conditions were appalling with filthy food provided by some army contractors who had evidently had their hands greased by "Q" Dept of the Portsmouth garrison; the food was badly cooked and uneatable and served up on dirty crockery by lousy waiters who ought to have been in the army. Some days we had to kick the waiters out they were so insolent; and a couple in particular were cleared out bag and baggage by the orderly officers one night and refused re-admittance to camp and had to spend the night on the road. The G.O.C. Portsmouth would not allow evening leave so we could not get our bellies filled in Portsmouth and we had to put up with things. There was nearly a mutiny and reports got to Parliament about the scandal. Capt. Fairbrother was the chief instructor and had every sympathy with us but could do nothing. The course was held at Fort Purbrook, Cosham; we were quartered in the fort and messed in tents outside. The fort like those at Dover was obsolete but very interesting as showing us what was thought the last word in field defences about 50 years previous. After the course, where in spite of all I had obtained an excellent report, I had leave and returned to the 13th Reserve Battalion who, worst luck, had moved to Blandford and were in hutments about four miles from anywhere. Only a few days spent here and then was sent to 12th Reserve Battalion at Bovington Camp, Wool, where another general course was being held for surplus officers. This was a vast improvement on Blandford, as there were many days out on tactical exercises and sports for officers.

❖

December

Just before Christmas I was sent to the depot at Budbrooke, Warwick to help with the Lord Derby recruiting scheme and made arrangements to live at home and travel up to Warwick each morning; but this did not last more than three or four days as the C.O. discovered that I should have gone to Rugby on a similar job; so to Rugby I went. Here I lived in apartments of the very best, but work at the drill hall was very boring and I spent day after day sorting attestation papers etc.

The C.O. was a dear old chap but had both feet nearly in the grave and was just doing his last bit. However it was at any rate much better than

Warwick; where I had to lunch with Col. Brown, Mrs Brown and a few more blue-blooded county people who talked over my head about horses and hunting etc.

❖

Charles Lander (seated) with who was to be his Best Man in 1918,
Lt F.P. Smith who also survived the war.
Taken in 1915 at the premises of Whitlock's Photo Studio which was
located in the Great Western Arcade in Birmingham.
Author's collection.

1916

Men of the Royal Warwickshire Regiment. July, 1916.
Dept. of National Defence/Library and Archives Canada/PA-000100.

February

While at Rugby I fell ill with jaundice and had to go home for nearly six weeks and so lost my job. When fit again I returned to the 13th Reserve Battalion at Blandford and spent the rest of my time in England as officer in charge of the butts on the rifle range; a job on my own with no one to interfere. The only diversion of interest was being sent to Warwick occasionally to fetch drafts of recruits. These trips, for which I had to thank my friend the adjutant, Capt. Masters, enabled me to slip in home for the evening on the way.

❖

April 16th

Being at home one weekend on leave, very peaceful and very much in love, a telegram arrived giving orders to proceed overseas. I must confess that rather a lump developed in my throat and all sorts of fears ran through my mind of what the future had in store for me: whether this was to be my last afternoon in the old house. Fortunately H. Allenby dropped in for tea and sentimentalities were forgotten. The morning came and I said goodbye. A very difficult job really. Mother, Dorothy (Doris) and Muriel to see me off.

❖

April 17th

Leaving New Street about noon I arrived at Blandford about 5pm and reported to the adjutant who said, "Go on leave and report to embarkation officers at Folkestone on the 20th." But as it would have meant goodbye all over again, I decided to pack my things, settle up and go to London for the remaining three days instead of home.

❖

April 20th

About 2pm I arrived at Boulogne and as I stepped on the quay I realised that this was the beginning of a new life; full of thrills and new interest. There were thousands of khaki-clad soldiers about of all units; new drafts, officers and men returning from leave; red tabs and blue tabs and brass hats by the score all reporting to the R.T.O. for instructions. The staff officers were mostly met by cars from their units and were soon away. The new drafts were sorted out and marched to a compound by the docks to await further movement orders. Young subalterns like myself were allowed out into the town till midnight when we had to report to the R.T.O. at the town station for a train to the base camp.

Making friends with a few others of my own sort we strolled into the town, first of all to look for a decent hotel and a meal. We sampled the best of fare at a posh hotel facing the quay and were presented with a bill at the end about a yard long. I think that the meal cost us about 30/- each (27fr to £1) being green we had ordered from the à la carte and had been charged for everything put on the table whether sampled or not. We created and the waiter fetched the manager who spoke volumes with actions, but as none of us could speak French and conversation was getting overheated we of course had to pay when the manager threatened to fetch the gendarmes – but we told the manager what he and all Frenchmen were.

❖

April 21st

About midnight we entrained and arrived at the base depot (29 I.B.D.) Etaples about 3am next morning, where we spent a few boring days doing useless parades, gas courses etc., being subject to the most rigorous discipline; owing no doubt to the fools who had gone before.

❖

April 24th

At last my name appeared in orders to proceed to the 10th R Wks R and leaving early on the morning of 24th April proceeded by train via St Omer, Hazebrouck, Bergotte and Aire to join my battalion who were then in billets in the village of Witterness. To me the train journey was full of interest; some of the other officers travelling with me had been out before and didn't forget to let me know of the places and females they had been acquainted with. We changed at a little place called Bergotte where we just had time to get some lunch of egg and chips at an estaminet. The French railways amazed us they seemed so antiquated; the permanent way was all overgrown with weeds, there are no platforms to most of the stations and the engines cough and burn patent fuel and the porters look like tramps and any old time does for the train to depart. The town of Aire had not then been touched by the war and looked very prosperous as I walked through on my way back to battalion H.Q. On reporting to Capt. Briscoe (adjutant) I was introduced to Lt-Col. R.M. Heath, D.S.O. and posted to "D" Company (Capt. A.N. Henderson).

Company H.Q. and mess were in the spacious kitchen of a prosperous farmhouse, the officers sleeping out at some nearby house.

The company officers at this time were:

Capt. A.N. Henderson	Killed 23/7/16 -
	(when in Comm of Bn at Bazentin le Petit
	act Lt-Col.)
2nd-Lt Rainbow	Killed 22/7/16
2nd-Lt Rance	To England wounded 11/15
2nd-Lt Browne	To England wounded 3/7/16
2nd-Lt Woodbridge	Killed 15/9/16
2nd-Lt Hart	Killed 30/7/16
2nd-Lt Bishop	To England sick 11/16
Lt Brindley	
2nd-Lt Lander	

The day I arrived Capt. Henderson must have been in trouble with his liver for within a few hours of joining the company I chanced to pick up a trench map which was lying about and Henderson barked 'put that down.' I apologised and shrivelled up somewhat but rallied on noticing that the others winked at me. They informed me later that only company commanders had maps of the line and that the old man would be all right when he got to know me. All the same I felt it was a bad start and was scared of him for days afterwards: until one day an opportunity came to get his confidence. We were marching by company to a rifle range and I noticed that the captain was leading us astray (couldn't read his map). I thought – shall I let the old devil make himself the laughing stock of the battalion, or shall I risk his wrath and suggest that he was not doing the best way? I decided that his mistake might reflect on the other officers of the company also and so, after making quite sure I was really right, I ran to the head of the company and told the old chap. He spluttered and spit a bit but after he had consulted 2nd-Lt Woodbridge who was with him, he halted the company.

The other officers came up and we had a smoke and talked it over and the result was: 'Well done Lander' and we about turned. Ever after we were the best of pals.

About a couple of weeks were spent here training. The weather was beautiful and the country at its best and we fed like fighting cocks. Before leaving Witterness, Henderson celebrated his 50th birthday; we all had a great binge at his expense. Before we adjourned, the captain pitched his out of the window. I managed to hold mine until I reached my billet; then I threw up and had a rotten night. Never again did I mix my drinks or take too much, it never was worth it.

❖

May 7th

About 7pm on 7/5/16 the battalion entrained at Aire for a journey south; going by way of Bethune, St Pol and Amiens detraining early morning of the 8/5/16 at Cagny on the outskirts of Amiens and marched to billets at Vignacourt, arriving 1pm, a long straggling village in the open rolling country peculiar to the Somme area. The surrounding fields and roads being unfenced and the only trees in the district seemed all gathered together inwards which stood out as landmarks; the few farms in the district were far between and the peasants' houses usually clustered together as small villages were only made of beams with plaster or mud between with floors of beaten earth. Here we did more training, chiefly by companies with occasional route marches and bathing parades in the river Somme. The river district was very beautiful, the river here consisting of a number of deep and dark pools of icy cold water, with marshy ground covered with rushes and iris between, the river proper wending between with an almost imperceptible flow. There were at this time of the year myriads of highly coloured butterflies and dragonflies about. Great caution had to be taken at these bathing parades to ensure the safety of the non-swimmers; the experts had to look on while the novices had their dip first.

While at Vignacourt we had some very fine shows given by a divisional concert party called the "Tykes"; a really first class show, which was really well patronised. During mess one evening, great amusement was caused by 2nd-Lt Woodbridge receiving a chit from the adjutant to the effect that the C.O. considered that his hat was "neither military or civil and was also filthy dirty".

Capt. Westwood also caused considerable amusement among officers by appearing on parade in pyjamas. Most company commanders were in the habit of cutting early morning parade; on this particular morning the C.O. appeared, and Westwood's servant warned him just in time to pull on a pair of trench boots and a greatcoat; and although Col. Heath stood talking to him for some considerable time he never noticed the tops of his pyjamas above his boots. The only other times Heath's eagle eye was known to miss anything was when he inspected transport to look for a certain gramophone which always appeared at each new billeting place. Time after time it had appeared in orders before a move: "that all surplus kit and musical instruments were to be dumped". He had the officers' kit weighed and inspected all lumber but the gramophone still survived.

❖

May 30th

A further move, this time for divisional training near St Riquier. We marched to these new billets in St Riquier going via St Omer. The divisional training consisting chiefly of elaborate field days with special instructions as to what was expected of us in the coming offensive; (date as yet unknown). Our division (19th) was to be a flying column - after the line was broken! And our advance was to be rapid – very rapid – at least 10km a day; everyone was optimistic, particularly the staff. We had a demonstration of a battery of Stokes guns firing rapid, just to shew (*sic*) us that nothing could live in their fire, to say nothing of our artillery, mines and machine guns etc. In fact, all we had to do would be to collect up the remains of the Boche outposts and advance again next day and so on and on.

Much amusement was caused here at mess one evening; by 2nd-Lt Rainbow's effort to drink half a bottle of Cointreau for a wager of 60fr; and this was after he had already done himself quite well at dinner with other drinks. He was successful of course; nothing would beat him in this line, but I was his unfortunate companion in billets. I managed to get him home and to steer him through Madame's bedroom without any too suggestive a conversation with her, but was not able to undress him; and down he flopped on his bed, dead to the wide world. A little after midnight "crash" went the window, and, getting up with a start, I discovered friend Rainbow with his head through the broken window, catting and groaning for all he was worth.

Before we left St Riquier Capt. Henderson and Capt. Shaw put up their crowns, two dud majors having been sent home, presumably on an adverse report being sent to the higher command about them by Lt-Col. Heath. One, Maj. Simnot, was a windy old devil who stuttered very badly, a regular from the retired list. He was chiefly noted for his speed in leaving the trenches, and for choking off young subalterns on parade to cover up his own ignorance. On one occasion he called Lt Marsden a "bl-o-ody ma-hutton headed sa-hod". The other senior officer to go was Maj. Taylor (Tubby) another old regular. He also suffered from an impediment in his speech, owing to a constipated nose. He was not windy but a glutton, whose belly was his first consideration, and his eyes nearly came out of his head every time a subaltern in his mess had a parcel from home. They were both thoroughly inefficient and would have been a common danger, had we had to go into a real attack with them.

———————— ❖ ————————

June 10th

Today we marched back to Vignacourt and occupied the same billets as before. A final polish up and then on the 13/6/16 marched to Rainneville; staying here only one night in billets; continued our march on 14/6/16 going via St Gratien and Franvillier to billets in Albert.

The day before we left Vignacourt Capt. Briscoe (adjutant) asked me to take charge of the signallers. I told him how little I knew about signalling, but he said it was chiefly for discipline, as they had become rather slack having no officer directly responsible.

With some regret I left the company; the change-over meant messing at H.Q. mess with Lt Col. Heath, Capt. Briscoe (adjutant), Dr Herd (M.O.), Lt Bass (M.G.O.) and Lt Brindley (assistant adjutant). Being very junior and with no active service experience I was not at all comfortable in my new quarters; they were very stodgy owing to the presence of the C.O. who very rarely addressed any remark to me, except occasionally to ask me a question, which I usually found very difficult to answer. He always appeared to be trying to test me, and it was a long time before I got over this feeling; and many a time I wished myself back in the free and easy company mess. Despite these drawbacks, there is no doubt that my new job gave me a slightly better chance of living to the end of the war; and it certainly gave me a greater knowledge of the tactical situation, for I always kept my ears open and said little.

Albert, at this time, was hardly touched by shell fire; the chief damage had been to the cathedral in the square and to a few houses on the German side of the town on the Bapaume Road. There were still a few civilians living in the town – probably not more than 500 – who were chiefly occupied in selling eatables to the troops; and picture postcards were being sold in great quantity. These civilians who remained must have been piling up the brass, as there was at this time a great concentration of troops in the town and in billets or bivouacs close by. A couple of decent cafés for officers were open at certain times and much wine was being sold; and the fancy cakes they sold were much appreciated. Of course all this went on behind closed shutters as no increase in activity was to be known to the Boche: no light at night and as little movement as possible by day.

H.Q. mess was in a decent house near the railway station and during our stay there, not a single shell fell into the town to my knowledge. Occasionally a few heavies dropped in fields on the outskirts of the town, searching for our guns. They didn't shell the station sidings which seemed to us an obvious target. Old Fritz was lulling us into a false sense of security, making us believe that he was quite ignorant of the great concentration of troops and materials in the district.

❖

June 16th

The 16/6/16 was a red-letter day for me. I went for a Cook's tour of the front-line trenches. Reporting at the H.Q. of a brigade then in the line, we were supplied with guides. Starting off up the Bapaume Road towards La Boiselle, entering the communication trench on the right side of the road, we went forward and passed along the front line toward Authuille absorbing all the items of interest as they were pointed out to us, and incidentally absorbing a lot of whisky at each company H.Q. The ground to the front of us of course could only be viewed through a periscope but toward the north-west we could get a splendid view of the lines the other side of the valley over the Thiepval ridge. Both sides were particularly inactive today and I could only imagine what it would be like to be under fire. During our stay in Albert the battalions were supplying working parties each night and although I was attached to H.Q., I of course clicked for one of these jobs. Reporting to R.E. officers at the entrance to the communication trench on the Bapaume Road, our job this night was to carry forward trench mortar ammunition for the large 60-pounder stuff which had to be concealed at various places just behind the support line. Passing along the trenches we noticed the R.E. and their infantry working parties engaged on completing the galleries to the mines which were to go up on *the* day. Very laborious work this had been, as all the earth taken out had to be put in sand bags and removed some considerable distance each night. Being chalky soil, to have thrown it over the top of the trench would have given the operations away.

❖

June 22nd

Marched back to billets at Bresle, arriving about 9.30pm – a few more working parties and a bit more cleaning up. At Bresle a certain Capt. Sellex was taken on the strength he came to us from the Cameroons, and caused a sensation by reporting in drill uniform complete with pith helmet. This fellow was to cause the battalion a lot of amusement and not a little trouble. When we first saw him his face was all smashed about and his arm in a sling. He informed us that he had fallen out of the train and that he was suffering from malaria. He was tight of course; in fact, he was never really sober though he always put his condition down to fever, for which he took enormous quantities of quinine and whisky.

❖

June 26th

Operation orders were issued for the coming offensive. Only 50 per cent of the officers were to go into action the first day. The others, of whom I was one, were to go to transport lines on the Senlis Road, north of Millencourt. The 19th Division was to be in corps reserve (III Corps) of the Fourth Army. The other divisions of our corps were 34th Division on the right and 8th Division on the left. The 57th Brigade was the reserve brigade of 19th Division: brigade commander Brig.-Gen. Jeffreys, divisional commander Maj.-Gen. T. Bridges C.M.G., D.S.O.

❖

June 27th

Orders were issued for a move on the following evening, which was "Y" day.

❖

June 28th

The battalion started off to take up a position in corps reserve, and supernumerary officers went to transport lines as arranged. We had just broken away from the battalion when a dispatch rider arrived with a message for the C.O. The Battalion was about-turned and marched back to billets in Bresle, the explanation being that owing to the bad weather and the sodden state of the ground, zero hour had been postponed. We were not kept in suspense very long, for, on the evening of 29/6/16, battalion orders gave the information that the 30/6/16 was to be "Y" day; so, on the evening of 30/6/16 the battalion really moved to its corps reserve positions, cheered on as they passed by all ranks of echelon "B".

❖

July 1st

The great day dawned, and those of us who had been left behind spent the greater part of the day on the high ground in front of Millencourt watching with glasses for any sign that would give us a clue to the progress of the battle.

❖

July 2nd

The day following was the same except that sausage balloons had sprung up by the dozen – German ones now, as well as our own. Our own balloons appeared to be in the same position as yesterday, and to the pessimists this looked very ominous, and our hearts began to sink.

❖

July 3rd

This morning was as yesterday; still no news but much speculation. During the afternoon a number of us were detailed to report to brigade H.Q. in the "Tara–Usna" line. Before moving off in battle order we handed to the quartermaster letters for home: last letters, which he understood were only to be posted if we were killed. What outpourings of love and sentiment had been put into these letters for by this time most of us were thoroughly worked up with the awful waiting.

At brigade H.Q. we were kept waiting for hours, sitting huddled up in the trenches nearby; and very little news of importance could we gather. At last the staff captain appeared and detailed a number of us to go on up to battalion H.Q. The few selected included Maj. Henderson. Those not selected were sent back to transport for yet another night.

Coming back on the Bapaume Road we met a number of our own wounded, some on stretchers and some walking, but all with trophies – chiefly helmets of the German guards – and they were all in the best of spirits. There were a number of German prisoners coming back too, though not as many as we should have liked to see. We learnt that Lt-Col. Heath had been wounded slightly in the leg and that our doctor Capt. Herd had been killed outside his aid post.

❖

July 4th

In the afternoon the remaining officers again had to report to brigade H.Q. where we waited some hours before being detailed for a job.

About 9.30pm my turn came and I found myself in charge of a rum and ration party for our battalion. I was given a guide and started off with my party up the communication trench which ran just north of the main Bapaume Road. The night was quite peaceful, with very few shells coming over – it seemed as if both sides were exhausted. There was, however, intermittent machine gun fire along the whole front: the result of jumpy nerves. Our trenches were very little knocked about by shell fire, but the conditions underfoot were very bad owing to some heavy showers we had had earlier in the day; in places the trench was quite 3 feet-deep in water and trench boards and other things were floating about.

It was very difficult to keep head and ration bags above water owing to the broken trench boards and the slippery nature of the chalky ground underneath.

We passed a few of our machine gun posts, all standing to, and some rather unpleasant sights as well. One in particular made me feel very sick. I slipped when wading through some water and my hand caught hold of something round and slimy, half submerged, which rolled over and shewed it to be the head of a dead British Tommy, whose lower portions were stuck in the slime or trench boards. This was the first dead body I had ever seen. When we arrived at what I presumed to be our old support line, our guide got out of the trench and we moved across the top toward the right. I now began to feel a little bit shaky, as the M.Gs appeared to be firing at us and stray bullets were flying about, and as it appeared to me in all directions. Of course, I had lost my bearings and was completely lost; I began to wonder whether our guide was lost also, but he was rather indignant when I mentioned to him that it seemed we were going too far to the right. We were now stumbling along for what seemed miles on slippery shell-torn ground through barbed wire and in and out of the remains of exceptionally deep trenches. We passed what our guide told us was the great mine crater, then of a sudden he stopped, saying, 'Battalion H.Q., Sir' and there was one of our sentries at the top of a dugout – a German dugout. Before I could get down, up popped Major Henderson looking very sleepy and untidy, without a hat or any equipment and his bit of hair all ruffled up on top. Reporting to him I told him what we had brought with us and ventured a few remarks. He was not a bit communicative; just said gruffly, 'Good, dump the stuff here, you will go to "A" Company taking two jars of rum: here's your company runner.'

Off I went again through the remains of an extraordinary trench system, built during the previous two years of trench warfare by the ever-industrious Boche. In all kinds of unexpected places were entrances to dugouts: very deep and spacious inside, mostly down about 20 steps, with two or three entrances to each, and opening out at the bottom into different compartments with rows of wire beds against each side of the walls. One could really sleep here in peace: no shells could penetrate to such a depth, but they were death traps to those who tarried below when our fellows came over and started to sling bombs down them.

As we passed on toward our front line we noticed a number of German dead about, and of course bodies of our own infantry. The place was littered with equipment, rifles, stick bombs, boxes of S.A.A. and other trench stores.

When we found our company we noticed that they were all standing to with fixed bayonets and all on the qui vive; our men were packed shoulder-to-shoulder in a bit of trench no more than knee deep and with no protection in front, except perhaps a couple of strands of wire in places. The company commander gave me our position which was approximately across the eastern end of the village of La Boisselle.

'We are now by the church,' he said. I took his word for it. Not a stone remained of the village; it was just a mass of rubble, and our narrow trench was dug in and out wherever it had been possible to dig. My first job was to go round with the C.S.M. and dish out a tot of rum to each man – and help to collect spare bandoliers of ammunition off the dead bodies we could find.

As dawn broke I was able to take stock of the situation. We had no protection in front and hardly any field of fire (not more than 20x on our company front), the ground having been won yard by yard by hand-to-hand fighting with bombs. As night fell they just dug in as best they could on the position gained. The Germans in places were not more than ten yards away and at times we saw some daring fellows dash across a gap in their broken trenches, and once one of the devils was seen to wriggle on his belly along in front of us not five yards away. I think he had been listening all night and as dawn was breaking tried to wriggle back home again, as he went behind a mound of earth we lobbed a mills bomb at him and got cursed for trying to stir up trouble.

We were in full view of Ovillers La Boisselle, which place was on higher ground away to our left front, and if we dared to stand upright a sniper let fly so we had to move about very warily. Our own dead lay pretty thick about us: some horrible sights, Lord knows what they would look like in a few days after the summer sun had got at them.

Towards our rear we could trace the Albert to Bapaume Road, now almost completely grass-grown, while by the side of the road could be made out the remains of a French ammunition cart: a relic of the days in 1914 when the French were pressing back the Germans after the battle of the Marne. We were not worried much by shell fire and all the stuff that came over was small and dropped on the battalion on our right – lucky for us.

❖

July 5th

Before midday orders came about a relief. Guides were sent back and very soon our relief arrived and the changeover was completed without any loss. We moved back along a trench which had been dug during the night to connect us up to our old front line. From this trench we could see away to the north hundreds of bodies hung up on our own barbed wire. I do not believe any of our troops had got beyond for when the attack started the Boche was just waiting ready and mowed them down with M.G. fire. We learnt later that when the mine went up, the Boche was first to man the crater, he had just been waiting and knew the exact time of the attack, so all our secret preparations had been in vain.

To the junior infantry officers it appeared that the greatest fault of the attack had been lack of artillery preparation. Trenches and wire which were supposed to be blotted out by our fire were in reality hardly touched. The speed of the advance had been against us; it was not possible for infantry heavily laden as they were with extra S.A.A., bombs, picks and shovels to move at the rate of 100 yards a minute, they simply could not keep up. And the artillery fire of ours of course lifted off the Boche front line before our chaps had cleared our wire because proper use was not made of the cover our own trenches would give – and the great mass of our attack was moved to the attack over the top of our trench system in artillery formation and was mown down before even reaching our own front line. The cause of excessive losses among officers was the fact that they wore knee breeches and, as we afterwards learnt from prisoners, were easily discernable by the German snipers. Another cause of excessive losses from the German infantry fire was the fact that we had all gone into action wearing a piece of yellow material fastened over our haversacks which were worn on the back (battle order). The idea was that after we had taken the German position and were lying down in a firing position or digging in, our aeroplanes as they came over would more easily be able to plot on their maps the limit of our advance. A very good idea if the attack had been the success anticipated (the III Corps' first objective had been Pozières) but when things went wrong and the ground had to be won yard by yard with the aid of bomb and bayonet, one can imagine the glorious target we all were, should we for a moment face the wrong way. The remains of the battalion on being relieved waited until dusk in the trenches about the Tara–Usna line and then moved by platoons to billets for the night on the outskirts of Albert on the Amiens Road. We did look a lot of guys, all filthy dirty and with four days' growth of beard; and most of the men had managed to scrounge some souvenirs, chiefly German helmets, which they slung on the ends of their rifles. I wonder how many of these found their way to Blighty. These billets were fine. H.Q. was in a large private house from which the inhabitants had evidently only lately departed as there was a quantity of furniture, crockery and heaps of books still here; and I must confess that when we left for Millencourt in the morning of 6/7/16 I also had a few souvenirs – a set of leather-bound prayer books. One still survives and is in use today, nearly 20 years after.

❖

July 7th

Left billets in Millencourt and marched to Henecourt Wood where we bivouacked for the night.

❖

July 8th

Marched back to billets in Millencourt; why? Lord only knows. We spent nearly two weeks here cleaning up and refitting, a real rest, no working parties to worry us.

❖

July 19th

Marched in the evening (all in battle order) to a field about ¼ mile north-west of Fricourt where we bivouacked for the night, again within range of the German guns, but were left undisturbed.

❖

July 20th

Received orders to reconnoitre trench system in Mametz Wood where the Battalion were moved after dark to be in brigade reserve. We went off – Mr Gott , myself and a couple of runners proceeding via Fricourt village and up the valley to Mametz Wood. We entered the wood where the undergrowth was extremely thick and got on to a grass clearing which took us to the northern end of the wood where the trenches were that we had to reconnoitre. We were horribly scared once or twice by a few 5 .9s which the Germans dropped occasionally on the wood making it reverberate from end to end; very uncanny and terrifying as up to the present we had not experienced the sensation of being shelled in a thick wood, where there was no cover and we were expecting any moment to be felled by a falling tree. The trenches we had to inspect and portion out to the companies, were in places choc full of German and British dead and the ground round about us was littered with them also. There had evidently been a terrific hand-to-hand fighting here on the 14th and the dead were still unburied and in a horrible state of decomposition and covered with flies, who were having a real good summer. We came back another way, along the valley south-east of the wood. The ground was very little cut up and there was a great concentration of artillery here – we could see the remains of the villages of Montauban and Mametz; they were not levelled to the ground as was La Boiselle and the churches could still be distinguished.

As I was leaving Mametz Wood a gunner on horseback approached. He was a sorry mess, covered with blood from head to foot. He wanted me to shoot his horse, the poor thing had stopped one in the neck and every time it took a step and moved its head the blood gushed out and smothered itself and its rider. This was a problem; I didn't know what to do. I was not very handy with a revolver and thought if I shot the poor beast it might take half a dozen shots as I didn't want to get too near and get all bloody myself. Then I thought perhaps it was not a serious wound for a horse (knowing nothing about horses) and didn't want to destroy a fine beast worth perhaps £60, so explained this to the gunner and told him to carry on till he met one of his own officers who would know something about horses and whether it could be patched up. He didn't have to go far, for the first gunner officer he met soon despatched the poor beast: one shot in the forehead and it sank to its knees and passed out.

Arriving back at battalion H.Q. I reported to the C.O. (Lt-Col. Henderson) and that same evening was detailed to guide the battalion to the position we had reconnoitred that morning. I was attached to battalion H.Q. as liaison officer to keep in touch with the troops on our right flank. The battalion H.Q. here was in an old German shelter by the side of a battery of 8-inch guns half dismantled; probably it had been the H.Q. of the German battery commander. The night passed quietly enough, the only distraction being the appearance at H.Q. of Capt. Sellex; half canned and quite crazy.

He complained that the trenches I had allotted to his company were full of dead and stinking. 'Then bury them,' said the C.O, and off went poor old Sellex muttering.

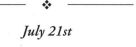

July 21st

As soon as day dawned I wandered out to take stock of our situation; it was a lovely morning and heaps of birds were chirping in the wood which was very little blown about, the undergrowth being very thick. The German battery was discovered to be four Russian pieces: they had not been damaged by our fire but were in process of being dismantled by the Germans who had evidently beat a very hasty retreat. On the northern edge of the wood were other German field pieces with their limbers blown to pieces as they were being withdrawn; and German gunners and their horses lying half-buried by the side. Toward the villages of Bazentin le Petit and le Grand all was quiet; no indication of the terrible time we were to experience on the morrow.

This morning I had orders to report on the positions held to our front and on our right flank. The brigade was evidently pretty hazy as to the present dispositions of their own and neighbouring units. Taking with me an intelligent N.C.O. and two runners we proceeded round the front and support lines in front of Bazentin le Petit and Bazentin le Grand. Fortunately the Boche were not at all active this morning and I was able to make a very accurate report, and was complimented on my work by the C.O. As far as I can remember – after so many years – our front on this particular morning was in front of the northern edge of Bazentin le Petit to about 8 b 2.8 then S.E. to road 8 b 6.2 then about E. across roads and in front of wood and windmill to about 9 b 2.3 where we joined up with division on our right; we also had machine gun posts at points (cross roads) 58 and 95. There was a battalion H.Q. in village at 8 b 1.4 and another in chalk pit by cemetery at 8 b 8.1. Most of the German shells were falling about the windmill and we gave this most unhealthy spot a wide berth; the rest of our front was comparatively quiet. We were particularly struck with the enormous natural as well as artificial strength of the German position about Bazentin le Grand which commanded the valley toward Mametz and Fricourt. There was an enormous quantity of German automatic rifles about but very few German dead, also very few of ours; the attack which our forces had launched here on the 14th inst must have taken the enemy by surprise.

Today there was a large party of the Lifeguards in Mametz Wood. They were burying the dead; a gruesome job in this hot weather. This was about the only useful job that could be found for our cavalry and so things remained for about two years, though they were repeatedly brought up near the front in the hope that the infantry might break through.

During the night when sharing a dugout with the M.O., I experienced an awful nightmare and woke to find the dugout on fire and full of smoke. In the scramble to get out I badly damaged a foot and had to change jobs with J. Feast for the rest of this tour as it entailed less walking. My job now was liaison officer to brigade.

❖

July 22nd

The next day passed peacefully until late in the evening when there was a hasty call for company commanders and orders were given for an immediate attack. Breeze up. What a hope? There was none from the first; less than an hour to zero, and the companies had to be got into position in the dark, over ground not known by their officers, no reconnaissance being possible in the time. They moved off followed by Battalion H.Q. Three companies went past the cemetery before they were to deploy, the left company by way of the road through Bazentin le Petit, battalion H.Q. following. Attack timed for 11.15pm. Before we reached the village hell was let loose; our guns opened up and the Germans were quick to reply. Our poor bloody infantry stopped the lot. Those in front got held up, we did not know why, and those behind cursed them for not getting on, while we all hugged the bank at the side of the road (Bazentin le Petit main street) for what protection it would offer. When we did get a move on we passed smouldering masses of our own dead and dying, the German H.E. bursting among them having set fire to their clothing. It took us an eternity to find the entrance to what was to be H.Q. dugout, crawling on our bellies among the remains of the village and trying to bury ourselves in the ground each time a salvo came over.

H.Q. dugout was a fine place: big enough to give cover for at least 100 men. There were two entrances fortunately down about 20 steps; the only snag being that the eastern entrance had a M.G. trained on it from what appeared to be the direction of High Wood, though I doubt if it was really so far away. Every few minutes throughout the night a short burst of bullets would bury themselves in the ground round the top step. About midnight the C.O. went out to see how things were going leaving Mr Bishop, Feast and myself at H.Q. Shortly after the C.O. had gone Sgt Leech arrived with an awful tale of woe. "D" Company, he said, was lost somewhere: no officers left and he had come for instructions. The only thing to do was for me to go back with him and find them, so after a hasty perusal of the map I went, alternately crawling and running after the sergeant-major. We found the remnants of "D" Company on the road by the cemetery and we guided them up to the spot where they were to have gone over about two hours before. Here there was an indescribable mess on the road between cross roads at point 58 and point 3 c 2.2. Dead and dying lay sprawling across the road and the battalion or its remains lay three or four deep on the side of the road, apparently too scared to even dig in for anyone standing upright was sure to be hit by streams of machine gun bullets from the direction of High Wood, taking us in enfilade.

I enquired for an officer and the first we came across was that dam' fool Capt. Sellex (O.C. "D" Company). He had arrived at the jumping-off place but minus his company. I tried to get Sellex to tell me the situation in front but he was far too tight; all I could get out of him was 'The sh-sh shycolgical moment has gone, but I'm ready to go over with anybody'. The din of battle was so great that I had to lie by his side and literally bawl in his ear, telling him to pull himself together and get his men dug in as it only wanted about an hour to daylight. I then went along the line to see what other officers were left and ran across a major of the North Staffordshire Regiment. We talked over the situation and decided it was quite hopeless to try to carry on the attack, and to get cover and some sort of defensive line before daylight was the only thing to do. We found a few more junior officers who had survived and I left them to sort out the mess and get dug in, while my runners and I made off for battalion H.Q. to report the situation. This was not so easy; we had nothing to guide us, not having seen the position of H.Q. in daylight. It was a most nerve-racking experience trying to find a hole somewhere in Bazentin, all the time dodging shell and M.G. fire. It was nearly daylight when we arrived.

———— ❖ ————

July 23rd

When we got to H.Q. the C.O. had not arrived and we thought he had gone west, especially as we recalled a rather curious remark he had made earlier that night. When J. Feast and myself were preparing to go out for information he had stopped us saying, 'No, I will go myself, I have lived my life.' We three junior subalterns at H.Q. now began to feel our responsibility and didn't know what to do for the best; the situation was so black and we were sure old Fritz would counter-attack us on the morning, so we sent a note to Lt Westwood telling him he was senior and to do what he thought best (the original note from my F.S. notebook I still have). This note was not strictly truthful as Capt. Sellex was senior and I knew where to find him but we three were unanimous in our opinion that it would be madness to let a drunken sop like Sellex have command of the battalion. We had no sooner sent the note than the C.O. returned looking very worried. It was bad luck that the first time he should take the battalion into an action things should go so bad and no fault of his. He complimented me on getting "D" Company into action and said we had done quite right with regards to Sellex.

The day dawned and the shelling gradually died down and we swilled down a hasty meal, though our appetites were far from good. It had been an awful night even for those left in H.Q. dugout; deep down though we were, our candles were continually being put out by the concussion of heavy shell bursting on top, and time after time a shell would burst in one or other of the entrances and piles of earth and stinking fumes poured down the steps. Most of the night had been spent in gas helmets, continuously working to keep a passage open up the steps as we were all fearful lest we should get buried alive. About 9am the C.O. and I went on top to have a look round; he really wanted to find a place to do a job for himself but I dissuaded him from getting out on top as any movement drew fire. We were in full view of High Wood. He said he couldn't hold out any longer and told me to fetch the pioneer sergeant to dig out a latrine. I had barely descended more than two or three steps when a shell burst directly in the trench behind me. My heart nearly stopped beating for I knew without looking that it must have hit the C.O. One's ears get so keen that you can place the fall of a shell to a few feet. It must have been quite a few minutes before I could venture to look round and then it was as I expected: a pile of earth blocking the trench, the Colonel's tin hat on the parapet and on a closer look I could see the Colonel's bare back with a small hole that trickled blood, and his stomach was lying open and all mixed up with the fallen earth. A bloody mess, the shell had hit the side of the trench, exploded and blowing back had blown his gut right out. He was in a stooping position having had just a momentary warning of the shells approach, and stooping quickly had tried to escape his fate.

In the afternoon Capt. Dekayne came up from transport to take over command of the Battalion. This was luck for Dekayne; coming from the East African campaign he had been with us less than a couple of weeks and got command of a battalion without having been tried in any action on the Western Front. This afternoon I had to shew officers of the relieving battalion round the line; guides were sent back with them and as soon as it was dark we were relieved and went back to bivouac in Becourt Wood. With hearts in our mouths we filed back down the road in Bazentin; the scene of our terrible losses only the night before. A few days were spent in Becourt Wood, peaceful except at night when a few long-distance pip-squeaks dropped around us and disturbed our sleep. Fortunately most of them failed to explode and we suffered no casualties.

❖

July 29th

On the afternoon 29/7/16, Capt. (acting Lt-Col.) Dekayne led the battalion into action again; up to the old spot, Bazentin le Petit, to try again to take the German intermediate line. We all spent the night in the trenches we had started to dig on the morning of 24/7/16. Battalion H.Q. was situated in a bit of trench by the side of the road about 8 b 6.4. Today was my 23rd birthday; was it to be my last? I thought so for sure, and said my prayers pretty often, for battalion H.Q. came in for a hell of a shelling about midnight and having so little cover we consequently suffered heavily. The companies further forward suffered little, which was fortunate as their morale was not affected for the work they had to do the following evening. I lost my signal sergeant (Sgt Sergeant) and a number of other good lads. The sergeant had both his thighs smashed by a shell burst; we got him away on a stretcher, he was quite cheerfully smoking a fag, but passed away on the way down.

❖

July 30th

The morning brought the ration parties from transport together with two days' mail; there seemed to be an unusual number of parcels and we stuffed all day – it would have been a pity to get killed with a haversack still filled with good things. This morning the body of 2nd-Lt Rainbow was found still unburied where he had fallen on the 23/7/16. Other identifications were taken from bodies of our fellows killed·on the night of 23/24.

There was little to do until evening and as we waited anxiously for 6.10pm we watched with interest our 9.2 dropping at intervals on the German line we had to assault. We could actually see these shells falling and they appeared to be right on the spot.

Towards evening the C.O. moved battalion H.Q. up to a hole in support trench about 2 d 9.2 so as to be nearer to our companies.

After a short but very intensive bombardment (five minutes) our companies moved forward behind a creeping barrage put up by our 18-pounders. I believe that this was the first occasion in which British troops had used the creeping barrage and the rate of advance was only 100x in four minutes; only a quarter the speed that had been tried on July 1st. Our men and the troops on our right kept well under our bursting shrapnel and were into the German trenches before the Boche could get his M.G.'s into action; in fact before he realised that our shell-fire had passed his trench. The troops on our left (8th North Staffordshires) were too slow, did not keep up with our barrage and failed miserably with consequent heavy losses.

We at H.Q. had a most miserable time, waiting anxiously for news of the attack. Twice I went out, but it was certain death to get out of the trench, and had to return. The shelling was the most accurate and deadly we had ever experienced. Though the trench we were in was exceptionally deep, the dead lay thick at the bottom; one had actually to walk over corpses mixed with a few living specimens who had completely lost their nerve and with their last bit of energy were trying to scratch holes in the side of the trench for extra cover. Every few moments a peculiar kind of star shell would burst on the road lighting it up for the German M.G's to pour along it a stream of lead from the direction of High Wood.

After about three hours a runner got back from the companies with definite news. We had been successful but our left was in the air and bombs were wanted – hundreds of them. I had definite orders to go out and collect all stray men and bombs and lead them up to Capt. O'Donnel in the captured trench. I remember saying something about it being impossible just yet, but heard the C.O. ordering me, not asking me. So out I went and with the aid of the runner who had brought the message, managed to collect the necessary men with a few bombs, though we had to kick and threaten a few of the men as they were beyond reasoning with. We got them there and felt much better; it appeared quite safe in the captured trench and our spirits began to revive on seeing how cheery were the men who had done the job of taking the German intermediate line. Capt. O'Donnel and Mr Woodbridge were very elated at their success and were busy getting the line into a state of defence. We had of course lost a number of the best including Capt. Bird, M.C. who fell as they reached their objective. He was I think the finest officer the Battalion ever had and received a bar to his M.C. (posthumous award) for his effort this night.

When I arrived back at battalion H.Q. with full particulars as to the situation in our front line, I ventured to say things looked very hopeful but the C.O. did not agree; he was worried about our left being unprotected and immediately sent off to brigade for a working party. This party duly arrived and before daylight had dug a trench from the left of the captured line back to the road about S 3 c 3.3: pretty good work considering the stuff that was flying about. The rest of the night was rotten for those of us cooped up in the hole which served as H.Q. To make matters worse Mr Thornton came in raving with shell-shock, a complaint likely to sap the morale of those sharing the same apartment, and Mr Link had been dragged in badly hit in the back. His kidneys were all exposed and we couldn't find a dressing big enough to cover the hole, so we did the best we could and gave him morphine to keep him quiet. We got him away later and he survived.

❖

July 31st

Later in the day orders for relief came from brigade. What a relief! We nearly burst into song, but it was a long way out and there might be many a slip, so we just thought a lot and said little. Brigade orders were passed on to me after the C.O. had duly digested them. I was to organise the relief as far as the 10th R Wks R and attached troops were concerned so had to do some heavy thinking under exceptionally bad conditions. I had to make up my mind as to the safest way in: and in daylight too. I had to safeguard against unnecessary congestion in the trenches and we were packed like sardines already. The way out had been given us and though I disagreed with this, I had no option.

I duly reported, complete with my four guides, one from each company, who had satisfied me as to their intelligence. We met the staff captain at the north-west corner of Mametz Wood at 5pm as per orders, and the relief proceeded. We took them up past the cemetery and made good use of the trenches obtaining cover from view if not from fire. The Boche never suspected and all proceeded as arranged back to bivouac somewhere between Becourt and Fricourt about two miles east of Albert. After seeing all our men clear I deliberately disobeyed orders and my runner and I went out via trenches to the cemetery and then down the valley on the east side of Mametz Wood, as this appeared to us a much safer way though a good way further. We were last in camp; in fact we were so far behind the battalion that they had given us up as lost and we were too late for the soup. What a glorious sleep we had this night. It was a lovely summer night and news had got round that the division had finished with the Somme and were going back for a rest. We soon forgot the dead and the miseries of the past month and were soon full of beans – actually and literally.

--------- ❖ ---------

August 1st

The next day after a bit of a clean-up we marched to camp at Bresle passing once again through Albert.

--------- ❖ ---------

August 3rd

Two days later the 19th Division was moved up north. The 10th R Wks R entrained at Dernacourt on the 3/8/16 in the usual cattle trucks (hommes 40, chevaux 8) and proceeding via Corby, Amiens and Picquigny detrained at Longpré about 3pm and marched to billets at Vauchelles-les-Domart (about 25k north-west of Amiens). Here we spent three perfect days of ease and good living; the only parades were for a bathe in the Somme canal, the battalion parading in shirts and shorts on the first two days and then the C.O. got ticked off as some Johnny on the staff thought this dress unbecoming to soldiers of H.M. the King, so back we had to go into full kit. The whole battalion's sympathies were with the C.O. and the name of the staff was mud. One night at Vauchelles-les-Domart while sleeping, with Mr Thornton, we both had a startling experience. Whether it was the result of over indulgence or nervous reaction after the Somme battle I shall never know, but during the night we both got up in a sweat and a fright, seizing our revolvers and dashing for the window. There was no one there, yet we had both dreamt we were down a dugout and the Boche were coming down the steps to take us; on awaking in the dark the little light from the window appeared to us as the entrance of our dugout. It may have been some French peasant prowling round to see if he could pinch anything, but though we searched round and round the building we found no one, and in the morning on telling our story we were laughed at and told to take more water with it next time.

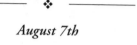

August 7th

On the morning of the 7/8/16 we proceeded up north, entraining at Longpré and proceeding via Abbeville, Boulogne and Calais; detraining at Bailleul to the village of Dranoutre in Belgium where we finished the night in a hutment camp.

August 8th

The same evening the battalion took over part of the line in front of Wytschaete–Messines Ridge. The troops we relieved were going south to carry on the Somme battle. Poor devils! Officers and N.C.Os. from each company having been up the line to reconnoitre earlier in the day, we moved off in the evening along Kemmel Road: didn't seem as though there was a war on – no firing, not a shell hole, no shattered trees – a bit of camouflage here and there across the road where it came in view of the German lines, or more probably to hide any movement from German sausage balloons. Civilians were still living within two miles of the front line and here within 2500x was the remains of an estaminet where women still served drinks at the entrance to one of our communication trenches. What a lovely war.

We entered the communication trench at Lindenhock corner, where we picked up rations and other stores and on we strolled down the most perfect communication trench 6 to 10 feet deep, with duckboards in A-1 condition, sides revetted, sometimes with wire and sometimes with brushwood. And above us and overhanging the trench, in places the vegetation was growing thick, and coloured with heaps of poppies and a few cornflowers. The trees were untouched by shell fire and the hedges grew thick having grown their own way undisturbed for over two years. This type of warfare was going to be a summer holiday by comparison with the month we had spent down south.

We took over, signed for the trench stores etc (without checking them) and after posting sentries, settled down for the night. In the morning we made out our front line to be from N 29d 8.5 to N 30c 4.0. We had two companies in the front line, one in support about 200x in rear and the other company in reserve on Rainsey Hill at N 34b 4.9; this spot was an old farm building concealed by a few bushes and trees. It had its own water supply and was entrenched so that it was a kind of redoubt; it had been christened Fort Edward. I remembered this spot during the tragic days of April 1918 and thought it might have been useful as a strong point to break up the German advance a little, but I was not allowed to use it: I suppose because it was isolated and most of us were so intent on keeping a continuous line. The front-line trenches were well built up and revetted with thousands of sand bags, well traversed and with good fire steps; and trench boards to keep one's feet dry. There were no dugouts as on the Somme, the ground being too wet, but corrugated iron shelters were built into the reverse side of trenches and well sand-bagged, giving cover only from whiz bangs (77mm). These acted as company H.Qs and as places for a few men to sleep. The support line was rotten, little better than a ditch; the system was well wired in front but had a poor field of fire. The companies were changed about every two or three days.

The battalion H.Q. were some elephant shelters built into the ground at approx N 33b 5.5; they were very spacious, with mess room, sleeping accommodation and kitchen. There was also a wonderful telephone exchange having buried cable to companies and brigades and to battalion H.Q.s on the right and left. As signal officer I had to take over the exchange; the wiring was a complete fog to me but my sergeant pulled me through.

While holding this stretch of line our casualties were few. German rifle grenades falling on our right caused the death of one man and splinters from bursting minenwerfer wounded a few. These flying pigs have a most terrifying effect on the troops. Though their actual destructive powers are not as great as one would expect from the ear-splitting crash they make on bursting, they affect the morale much more than does a 5.9 shell; this may be because you can see them travelling through the air and while trying to judge their fall and dodge them you get all worked up into an awful sweat. With care and good judgement you can dodge behind a traverse and be safe, but the difficulty is to keep the men from getting bunched up so that they may have freedom to move rapidly. When the Boche starts on you with these things from more than one direction at once and men shout 'Coming right – coming left', what is one to do? Fortunately they didn't, neither did they fire at night (when only a spark is visible) but always in the afternoon, just to spoil our cup of tea. We always tried to get our guns on to them but do not think our artillery even registered a hit. It was very difficult to place the position of these mortars as they were brought up on a trench railway and when our guns opened they either altered their position or shut up shop and started again later.

While in this sector of the front we had some fun with Capt. Sellex who suffered from malaria – so he said. His cure for this malady was two bottles of scotch and about 20 grains of quinine per day. We often had to hold him down on his bed with D.Ts and run the company affairs ourselves. We ought really to have split on him but he was so generous and good-natured when anything like sober that we tried to pull him through. In the end our help proved to be his ruin.

❖

August 26th

Received orders to report to brigade for a course of instruction on signalling under the brigade signals officer Lt Burnette. This course was great fun and a real holiday, billeted in Dranoutre near brigade H.Q. and messing with brigade no. 2, mess consisting of Lt Burnette (Sig. Off.), Lt Cran (bombs), Rev. Father Walker (padre) and a French interpreter – a very lively crew and no senior officer to cramp our style – we did ourselves well. The two months spent with 57th Infantry Brigade were the happiest times of all my army career. Most mornings and afternoons were spent on parade with the signallers (N.C.Os. and men) also under instruction. Little stunts were arranged well away from prying eyes: visits made to divisional signals, pigeons lofts, aerodromes etc. I was able to borrow a horse and learn to ride, though this accomplishment was not realised without making a fool of myself. The first time I mounted the old mare she took me the shortest way back to the stables and would have split my head on the stable door but for the fact that by this time I was hanging under the animal's neck; and all this in view of stable men and crowds of infantry splitting with laughter. Lt Burnette and I had many trips up the line to battalion H.Qs trotting up in great style to inspect communications, also visiting many other H.Qs where there was plenty to drink. The evenings were mostly spent visiting officers clubs or cafes in Bailleul. One evening in Bailleul I met Pte H. Ridgby of the fusiliers. They were going south; poor fellow went west a few days later in an attack at Longueval.

While with brigade, the 10th R Wks R lost three of their finest officers through foolhardiness. I think the whisky bottle had a lot to do with it; they were fooling about at night in no man's land strictly against orders and their loss took a lot of explaining to the higher command and caused special orders to be issued respecting patrols. Lt E.V. Briscoe (captain adjutant) was killed 27/8/16 while shewing a Canadian sergeant over no man's land. They evidently missed their direction and came upon a German post, were challenged and Briscoe was shot dead, his body falling into the German trench; the sergeant got back to tell the tale. Lt Briscoe's effects were later sent to the battalion by the Germans. I believe they were dropped over our lines by an aeroplane.

Early in September 2nd-Lt S.A.R. Woodbridge and Capt. O'Donnel, after making merry, went out on patrol in the region of the Bull ring; they lost their bearings and coming back to our line in front of the battalion on our right (8th North Staffordshires) were shot at by a sentry. 2nd-Lt Woodbridge got a bullet in the brain and O'Donnel, thinking they were in front of the Germans, doubled back and falling into the German lines was taken prisoner. Of course the 8th North Staffordshires should have been warned that we had a patrol out, then all would have been well, but when men are merry they are apt to neglect these details and be over-confident in themselves. 2nd-Lt Woodbridge lived for over a week with the bullet in his brain, getting home to London, though unconscious all the time. Capt. O'Donnel and I met again after the armistice; he said he had been treated extremely well, no doubt owing to a strange coincidence. Capt. O'Donnel said that the C.O. at the German battalion that had taken him prisoner happened to be a brother of a wounded German officer whom Capt. O'Donnel had taken prisoner on the 30th July/16 (at Bazentin). This wounded German officer had written to his brother telling him how kind O'Donnel had been to him and asking him to bear this in mind should any English officers ever fall to him.

--- ❖ ---

September 7th

Early in September, brigade H.Q. marched via Neuve Eglise and Le Romarin to new H.Q. at La Petite Monque Farm T23 d 8.8, the battalions holding the line in front of Hill 63 and Ploegsteert Wood. This sector (right of 19th Division front) was even more peaceful than the last. The ground right up to Hill 63 was still under cultivation and though the Boche strafed certain localities unmercifully the 10th R Wks R suffered no casualties. The 10th

R Wks R H.Q. were at Red Lodge T 18d 7.3. The chief danger spot was on the way up to Courte Dreve Farm where we had a battery which evidently worried the Boche judging by the attention he gave it. Hill 63 is very steep and thickly wooded on our side; it is particularly steep by Red Lodge rising approx 90 feet in 300 yards making this side of the hill safe from artillery fire other than the Howitzer. I only climbed up once just to view the German position; a very fine view particularly of the German trench system round Messines.

❖

September 11th

Brigade H.Q. moved to hutments in Romarin. A week later the division was withdrawn from the line and the 57th Brigade moved to billets in Outtersteene. This move was made on the morning of 19/9/16 and we signallers returned to our respective units while division was on the move.

❖

September 20th

The following morning we continued the march to the village of Borre (about 4km east by north of Hazebrouck) where "D" Company was billeted in a farm house.

❖

September 21st

The next day I returned again to brigade No. 2 mess and was billeted in the village of Borre. While at Borre, Lt Burnette went on leave and I was given temporary command of 57th Brigade Signals, the other signallers under instruction returning to their units.

During our stay here I spent a good deal of my spare time with "D" Company now under command of my friend F.P. Smith (Lt F.P. Smith joined battalion at Dranoutre 16/8/16) as Capt. Sellex had been put under arrest by Lt-Col. Heath (who had returned to battalion at end of August) for having lost (or pinched) about 2000fr of "D" Company's pay and mess account, and for conduct likely to cause a breach of military discipline. He had not only appeared in a state of intoxication on a brigade parade, but he had also publicly accused Sgt-Maj. Shoebottom of having pinched the messing money, and swiped him across the backside in front of the company on parade and sworn to break him. This was of course too much for such a disciplinarian as Lt-Col. Heath. The C.O. sent for F.P. Smith and created because he had not reported Capt. Sellex's conduct before; had he done so the C.O. could have removed him without resort to a court martial, presumably by an adverse report to higher authorities as in the case of Majors Simnot and Taylor earlier in the year. Capt. Sellex said he had lost the money while in the trenches before Messines as it was with other company effects in the mess box which was lost; however he could not account for the 2000fr which he had given Fr Walker to take home to England for him. Fr Walker went on leave and took this money quite innocently as he thought it was money Capt. Sellex had saved for Mrs Sellex. Two thousand fr (approximately £65) was a lot to have in hand and Sellex must have drawn from the Field Cashier much more than the actual requirements of the company for many weeks. It was also strictly against orders for anyone to take public money into action. The only other item of interest while stationed here was the parade of the whole 19th Division for inspection by King Albert of the Belgians who presented every man with a packet of cigarettes.

--- ❖ ---

October 6th

Brigade H.Q. paraded at 5.30am and marched to Bailleul station where we entrained about 9.30am and proceeded at the usual pace, travelling via Hazebrouck, St Pol and Frevent: detraining at Doullens about 5pm and marching to Sarton (6km SE of Doullens) where we were billeted for one night. Continuing our march next day at 2pm to St Leger les Authie where we settled down in billets for a few more days. The 10th R Wks R went to a hutment camp in the Bois de Warnimont; a filthy muddy hole.

The night at Sarton was full of interest there being an endless stream of infantry and transport passing throughout the night. A big movement of divisions was taking place. War-weary troops from the Somme area being relieved and we poor devils were shortly to take their place. There were no guns being moved as it had become the custom to relieve only the personnel of the artillery, the guns in action being handed over like trench stores to the relieving troops.

We were now once again in the barren country of the Somme with its lath and plaster houses and isolated villages and woods – and were expecting to go into action in front of Hebuterne. We got as far as making a reconnaissance, passing through Sailly-au-Bois to the trenches east of Hebuterne but never took over.

❖

October 16th

The division was moved again farther south and I had to bid farewell to brigade H.Q. and return to my unit on the 16/10/16 being posted to "D" Company (Lt F.P. Smith O.C.) thus ending the happiest ten weeks of all my army career.

While at St Leger I had had the opportunity of making a trip in an aeroplane (a BE2C). The purpose was to improve communication between the infantry in battle and the R.F.C. by means of ground signalling panel, flares etc. The former method had been used for some time but it was thought necessary that signal officers and N.C.Os. should view the methods from the airman's point of view. A splendid idea of course.

❖

October 17th

Left in charge of the rear party to clean up camp and hand over. I proceeded in the afternoon to join the battalion at Warloy-Baillon. Moving across country due south. We stayed here until the 21st just messing about. The officers continued their riding lessons started at Borre by Major Dakeyne; I think they were purely for his amusement as he delighted in bullying wretched officers who shewed no aptitude for the sport, making them take jumps on fiery steeds long before they could even sit upright in the saddle.

Brig.-Gen. Jeffreys also had a brainwave about this time. He applied for and obtained for each battalion a young officer promoted from the ranks of the guards for the purpose of smartening us up, the method being to teach us the goose step and slow march – quite all right for picked men like the guards on a posh parade ground, but an infantry battalion of a county regiment at this time contained all sorts and all sizes and the parade grounds about here at this time of the year were mostly a sea of mud. These benefits were extended to all junior officers who had to parade as a platoon and go through it like the men. Also to the amusement of Maj. Dakeyne.

❖

October 21st

We marched in battle order once again to bivouac in some brick fields somewhere between Seulis and Albert. The weather was appalling and the men had nothing but their ground sheets. Our spirits were sinking fast and sank right out when the C.O. called for all officers. We knew we were for it. Maps of the Thiepval area were given out and the C.O. explained the situation and orders for the relief we were to complete on the morrow. I was attached to "D" Company (F.P. Smith O.C.) and next morning the battalion marched once again through Albert to the old British front line in front of La Boiselle where we halted for some time while the company commanders went forward to view the line. In the afternoon they arrived back weary, filthy and fed up and after a few words of explanation to officers and N.C.Os. the companies again moved forward passing along between the old British and German front lines (of July 1/16). We had clear evidence of the terrible slaughter of July 1st and after; the dead had been buried where they fell – hundreds of them – marked sometimes by rough wooden crosses but mostly by rifles stuck bayonet first into the ground with a few words of identification written on a scrap of paper and stuck into the bolt. Large numbers of these bodies were only just covered and feet and legs still protruded above the ground with just a boot or fragment of sock remaining on the bones. These were the men of the new Kitchener armies, who, going over the top on the morning of July 1st had expected in a few more days to win the war. In spite of their dash none of the poor devils even got as far as the German wire.

On topping the high ground we could see across the valley, the renowned Thiepval ridge, stretching away east towards Courcelette, by now a vast sea of mud and slime, not a tree or a building of any form in sight: not a tree stump even a foot high, not a blade of grass. Winding through the valley from Aveluy to Mouquet Farm was the only road to feed this front. This road we had made out of a cart track by endless labour, and every week thousands of tons of metal and planks had to be laid in an endeavour to keep it above the slime. Even so, it was only passable by mules and infantry.

"D" Company passed two miserable days in reserve in Zollern redoubt between Thiepval and Mouquet Farm. The conditions for the men in the trenches were awful. We officers faired a little better as there was a very fine deep dug out, the usual German type but it stunk like hell. This was the company H.Q. Later we discovered the cause of the stink to be the dead body of a Boche, half decomposed under one of the beds. He must have been here since the redoubt was taken about a month before. We removed the body but not the smell. There was another dead Boche stuck in the mud of the trench; a most useful fellow – we used to catch hold of him to help pull ourselves out of the slime. He also acted as a guide and remained a well-known fixture here until one day the C.O. met him and created because he said it was bad for the morale of the troop troops; so this useful landmark had to be buried.

❖

October 24th

After two days here we returned to a hutment camp at Crucifix Corner, Aveluy and during the next three weeks spent our time doing two days in and two days out of the line at various spots on the divisional front; the best known positions being Regina, Hessian, Schwarben and Danube trenches. As the year wore on the conditions got worse and worse and we cursed these unnecessary reliefs: they just wore us out. The division must have lost half its strength through sickness and trench feet; the actual losses from fire were small, as quite half the shells that came over were duds, the ground being too soft to detonate them.

How we all cursed these reliefs; we would all have sooner stopped in the front line for a week. It was the going in and out up and down the trenches where the mud got thicker and deeper and more sticky every day, that wailed up and broke our hearts. On one occasion we were all shod in "boots, gum, thigh" but these only made matters worse, they stuck fast to the mud instead of to the feet and half the battalion lost their gum boots in the mud and finished in their stocking feet. With conditions like this should a man get wounded and fall in a hole, God help him if he had no pal near – he would surely drown or suffocate. Many a man who lagged behind must have passed out this way. With conditions such as these our morale suffered severely and had the Boche made any effort he would have encountered little opposition from our infantry who were half frozen with bellies empty and rifles choked with mud. Fortunately the German infantry left us in peace; conditions for them were probably just as bad.

When out at rest there was little peace, even the divisional band could not raise any enthusiasm. Everyone was lousy and spent most of their spare time scrapping the fat louse from the backs of their shirts and from the seams of their uniforms; some cracked the blighters between their thumb nails, others burnt them over a candle flame. The huts were very filthy and overcrowded, and the stink from the unwashed, the wet and steamy uniforms, mingled with foul tobacco smoke will never be forgotten. We paid several visits to the de-lousing station (Divisional baths at Bouzincourt) where all could get a hot bath and a change of clothes, the old ones being put into great cylinders where they were fumigated and dried ready for the next battalion.

❖

November 11th

On the 11/11/16 the great attack of the 63rd Naval Division and Newfoundlanders took place on our left at Beaumont-Hamel.

❖

November 14th

Officers were sent up from our brigade to reconnoitre a position astride the river Ancre then held by the 39th Division. We expected to take part in the continuation of the previous day's attack, but when we arrived back, full of knowledge, we found that orders had been altered and we stood fast until the 17th. Our afternoon reconnaissance had been wasted though very interesting.

Following our instructions our party proceeded up the valley of the Ancre, which is very pretty about here and was very little touched by shell fire, to Paisley Dump. Then on we walked along the edge of Thiepval Wood to Mill Road and the old German front line. The front line of the 118th Brigade was the Hansa line – a continuation of Stuff and Regina trenches whose aquaintance we had already made – the reserves being in the Strassburg line and Schwaben redoubt on top of Thiepval ridge.

While we were talking over the situation, a terrific barrage was put down by our guns on the left. To watch a sight like this and not be in it was great fun. This barrage was the most intense we had seen up to then – and appeared to be a vast blanket of white smoke with specks of fire, which was shrapnel bursting on a north – south line a few hundred yards west of Beaucourt-sur-Ancre and the noise a glorious soft rumble as of distant drums. Whether this barrage was put down to cover one of our attacks or in answer to an S.O.S. I do not know; anyway the Germans made a poor show in reply.

We expected trouble, but the only stuff that came our way were a few heavies sounding like express trains which fell near the mill, throwing up huge fountains of mud and water. We returned to camp by road west of the river and passed near Hamel a big dressing station working at full pressure. There were hundreds of cases passing through: rows of stretcher cases waiting their turn to be carved up and passed on to C.C.S. There were a number of German prisoners here. They were doing good work and returning time after time to the battlefield in search of stretcher cases. Other German wounded, were cheerfully giving a hand and chatting and smoking with our fellows as though they had always been the best of pals.

❖

November 16th

On the 16th November all officers were assembled and in was marched Capt. Sellex ("Hat off – quick march – halt – about turn".), standing facing all his brother officers while the C.O. read out the sentence of the court: the King had no further need of his services.

Lt Thornton was detailed to take Sellex down to the base and hand him over to the Provost Marshal. How I envied him; I think I envied them both. They were to have a nice little trip while we were to go through hell again, and many of us were not to come through.

❖

November 17th

We went up the line on the evening of the 17th November, conditions being worse than usual; it had been freezing for some days and the water which filled the shell-holes was frozen and covered with snow which had been falling at intervals since morning. We were allotted a sector of the divisional front which we had never seen in daylight, and without any previous reconnaissance had to attack at dawn the intricate German trench system in front of Grandcourt.

I was in charge of H.Q. Company as signal officer and sort of general odd man. Things started bad for me for on the way up my guide got himself lost somewhere in the wilderness between Zollern redoubt and Regina trench, so I cleared him off and taking the lead pushed on hoping for the best. We eventually struck Hessian trench and got our bearings, we were considerably out in our reckoning but eventually found a communication trench up to Regina trench (the front line) and moving to the left along this trench at last found the C.O. where this trench met the Lucky Way. This was the centre of the battalion front and Lt-Col. Heath fixed his H.Q. here. We had two companies on the right and two on the left; the 8th North Staffs and 8th Gloucesters were on our right and left respectively. When allotting H.Q. to their positions I made the horrible discovery that about a dozen of them were missing. 'Of course they are,' said the C.O. 'Haven't I always told you young officers to bring up the rear?'

I explained that our guide had lost us and had had to lead them to get here at all, but he wouldn't have it. He was very cool and more polite than usual – a very bad sign. Probably accounted for by the fact that on the way up before I had parted from his company he had fallen into a shell hole, breaking the ice and getting very wet up to his middle; and he didn't like to mess himself. I think this was the only occasion on which anyone had heard him swear; and then it was only a very muffled "damn it". The first thing to do then was to find the missing men and quickly too as I was due at brigade H.Q. at midnight to synchronise watches; quite a useless procedure really, as who could sleep through a barrage.

Fed up to the teeth I trudged back on my previous tracks, making enquires all the way and at last discovered the B-----s all nice and snug down a deep dug out in Hessian trench toasting themselves in front of a brazier. My language was a trifle hot and had I not been wounded next day should have crimed a few of them. They had made no real effort to find me thinking they had a good excuse and had I not found them they would have sheltered here until the attack was over – such was the spirit of the troops in November 1916. In spite of my troubles I arrived at brigade H.Q. at midnight 17/18, on time. The brigadier (Brig.-Gen. Jefferies) was in a wax as orders had just been received to make further alterations in the dispositions for the attack.

───────── ❖ ─────────

November 18th

While awaiting these new orders I heard the general ticking off division saying the notice was too short to alter present arrangements and that he couldn't take responsibility as he doubted whether he could let his front-line infantry know in time. Division said it was corps H.Q. and sympathised but could do nothing. The new orders were to the effect that a box barrage was to be put down round Grandcourt; hoping I suppose to hold the German garrison while our infantry passed on, thus sparing us the difficult task of village fighting. Then all we had to do was to take the garrison prisoners when they had been cut off – but it didn't work. It was of vital importance therefore that the 8th Gloucesters and the 10th R Wks R should all know in time, or they would have got cut up in our own barrage. There was still about five hours to zero but on such ground, in this weather, there was no time to spare. Corps H.Q. some 10 miles back nice and snug in a cosy billet evidently didn't appreciate our difficulties. In getting back with these important orders I tried to go straight on a compass bearing to save time and I was fortunate in my reckoning and struck Lucky Way trench almost dead on battalion H.Q. On the way I passed a number of tanks floundering along in the mud. They were to have assisted us in the attack but not one got beyond our own front line, the ground being quite impossible for them.

We lay out all night, wet and frozen almost stiff. I for one was in a frightful funk when at 6.10am our guns opened. Five minutes intensive bombardment and then at 6.15am the barrage moved slowly forward and in the dim light I saw our heavily laden infantry dragging themselves out of their trenches and shell holes to follow the bursting shrapnel which was their only guide. We waited as it seemed for an eternity expecting to get blown sky high at any moment. For some extraordinary reason the Boche never put down any counter barrage; we could hear his M.G. going strong and knew what that meant; our infantry had failed. It was fully 15 minutes before any shells came our way and then it was a feeble effort; mostly small stuff, the ground was so soft that their effect was very local. No doubt the reason for this slackness on the part of the German artillery, was the fact that all his guns would be north of the river and trained on the Beaumont Hamel front, where the fighting had been very severe the last days. The marshy river gave him a sure protection for his left flank.

As the day dawned we scanned the front for any sign of our infantry. They seemed to have vanished; and no runner came back with news for a long time. Mr Gott and I went forward down the road for a few hundred yards, but could see nothing and got sniped at; this didn't look as though our men had got into the German lines. When we got back, Maj. Fitzgerald (commanding two right companies) looking as though he had seen a ghost was talking to the C.O. I do not know what excuse Fitzgerald had made but heard the C.O. tell him to get all the men back to the position he had started from.

A little later Mr Gott (assistant adjutant) again went forward to investigate and as he didn't come back for some time I followed and not 20 yards from H.Q. came across his dead body lying flat in the trench. He had been sniped, shot through the brain, probably by the same sniper who had potted at us both earlier in the morning. When runners eventually got back from our left companies we learnt that they had been more successful and had taken most of their objective, but in the dark they had lost direction moving too far left and getting mixed up with the 8th Gloucesters who were also successful, so that between them, they held the German line from Grandcourt (Exclusive) to approx R 14b 9.1.

This made a bombing expedition necessary and I could feel the C.O. looking round for someone to lead this forlorn hope. These left companies of ours had only to extend their front another 300–400 yards to the right and it would squeeze the remaining Germans out of the ground between them and our two right companies. The job was mine, had not a piece of shrapnel hit me in the left hand just at the right moment. This changed the situation as far as I was concerned – no M.C. for me leading a forlorn hope when wounded; I awaited my opportunity and tactfully mentioned the fact to the C.O. that I had better have my hand dressed. When things quietened down and other wounded began to come back I pushed off with them down to the dressing station calling on the way at brigade H.Q. to tell the brigadier the situation. We were fortunate not to have been hit again on the way down for as soon as our little party got out of the Lucky Way we were fired at until we passed the top of the ridge; and our hearts settled down once more into their proper places. Our progress was very slow; the going was very bad for a wounded man. They had to be helped and rested continuously. Mr Stammers was with me; he was badly hit in the arm and bled like a stuck pig. We tried to get him to wait for a stretcher but he was too anxious to get out of it and struggled on till we came to a coffee stall where we all had a refresher. Here we left him with some R.A.M.C. bearers. At Aveluy I met Fr Walker (div. padre) and parting from the others went and had lunch with him. I was now full of beans again and after telling him all the news, got on a lorry and went to the advance dressing station near Bouzincourt. Later, after being dressed, I was sent with other slightly wounded by bus to the railhead at Acheux then by train to the casualty clearing station (C.C.S.) at Gezaincourt (2km south west of Doullens) arriving about 11.30pm. Here was a good meal awaiting us, a wash and a nice clean bed and happy dreams till about midday 19/11/16.

❖

November 19th

In the advance dressing station at Bouzincourt were a number of German wounded including one junior officer. They seemed a bit timid and our wounded were giving them cigarettes, tea and chocolate and doing their best to make them feel at home: truly a most extraordinary spirit of comradeship after all the bloody encounters of the past five months. I think the cause of our brigade failing to take the Grandcourt lines was entirely due to the failure of the higher command to appreciate the situation. In the first place, why persist in an attack when weather and ground conditions are hopeless? Even had we been successful it would have meant spending winter in low-lying ground instead of remaining on the high ground which we already held. The cause of failure, attributable more to our divisional staff, was the fact that we had not been able to make any reconnaissance. The units having been changed about after becoming acquainted with other ground over which they had expected to attack, caused the loss of the 8th North Staffords on our right including their C.O. and adjutant (Lt-Col. Parish). They had pushed off behind our barrage but failed to clean up some German dugouts on their flank. After they had passed, up came a handful of Germans with a couple of machine guns which took the Staffords in rear and these same M.Gs afterwards enfiladed our two right companies This would not have happened had we gone over in the Staffords position as originally arranged. We had spotted these dugouts and detailed two platoons to deal with them. Later we heard that an aerial reconnaissance reported having seen about 400 men marching towards Miraumont – they were the 8th North Staffords.

———— ❖ ————

November 20th

Entrained 2.30pm at Gezaincourt with about 500 other walking cases and arrived at Boulogne 5am.

———— ❖ ————

November 21st

Was sent to No.7 Stationary Hospital Boulogne. The most important question now was, could I get across the water with such a slight wound?

———— ❖ ————

November 25th

I was notified that I was to be evacuated the next day "if there was room on the boat"! Next morning I was advised to put my arm in a sling – to make it look a case and off I went to the quay to board a hospital ship to Blighty.

❖

November 26th

We had a good crossing, arriving at Dover about 12.30pm. The hospital train was waiting at the quay. While waiting to load up, many telegrams were sent home, though none of us could find out our destination. Late that night we came to the end of our journey which proved to be Manchester. The slightly wounded were hurried off in private cars. There was a cheering crowd at the station; we did feel foolish. During the war seeing hospital trains in, was always a first class entertainment. The officers went to Worsley Hall a few miles outside the city. The discipline was very strict; we were only allowed out in the afternoon and had to be in by 4.30pm. I suppose some fools had previously painted the town red and those coming after had to suffer. We were fed extraordinarily well; the food shortage had not yet been felt in military hospitals. I had a nasty shock when washing next day for I found that I was lousy, so had to spend the best part of the next few days hunting.

❖

November 29th

My people came to see me. They arrived when we were at lunch; the staff would not disturb me so strict were the regulations. I came out of the hall with a crowd of officers and I had changed so much they hardly knew me, for in spite of the trials of the past seven months I had fattened up considerably.

❖

December 2nd

I left hospital on 2/12/16 after the usual medical board and was granted six weeks leave of absence which carried me over Christmas. After the expiration of leave, my orders were to report to the 3rd Reserve Battalion R Wks R, then stationed at Parkhurst, Isle of Wight.

❖

Unit	From	To	Route	To pass starting point	at	Remarks
t.Qr. L.Coy + Bombers	ALBERT	BRESLE	via main ALBERT – AMIENS – road.	Xrd Junction – RUE TRAIRIES – RUE NEMOURES –	9.30pm	mess cart + mattire cart will follow H.Qrs.
"A" Coy					9.35pm	cooker + 1 baggage wagon will follow "A" Coy
"D" Coy					9.40pm	cooker + 1 baggage wagon will follow "D" Coy
C + B Coys			[route by marked route – signalled X'ds standing E304 then follow until then me Map.Ex–C3X via X roads Dug outs Qr near ALBERT]	Camp.	10.30pm	1 cooker will follow each Coy.

Battalion movements, June 1916. Author's collection.

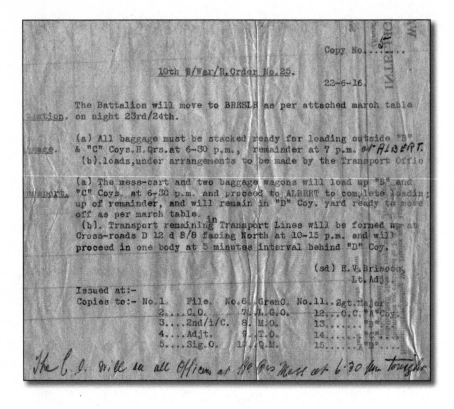

Brigade Order, 22nd June 1916. Author's collection.

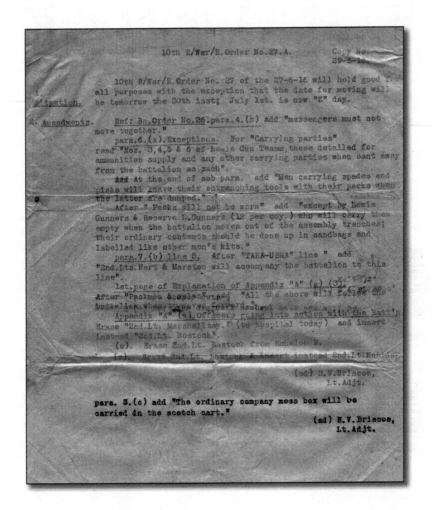

Brigade Order, 22nd June 1916. Author's collection.

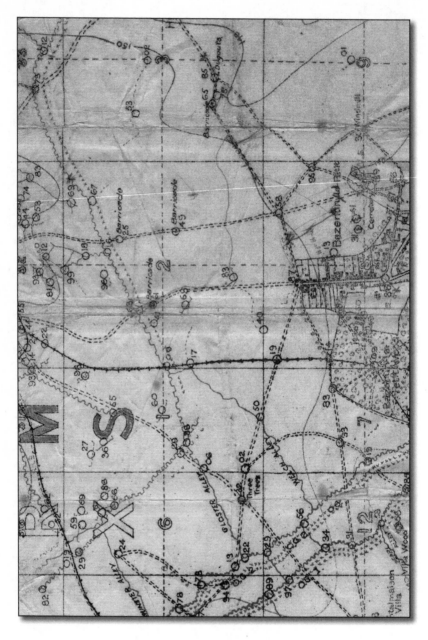

July 1916, area of operations: Bazentin & High Wood. Author's collection.

SECRET.   57th Brigade Order No. 31.   16-8-16.

1. The Heavy T.M.Battery will bombard the German front and new support lines today 16-8-16 from about N.36 a 7.3½. to N 36 a 6.6.

2. In conjunction with the fire of the H.T.M. ,the right group 19th Division R.F.A. on the treaches from N.36 a 9.5 to N 36 a 7½.8 The Medium T.M. on the German front line in front of Heavy T.M. objective.

3. The bombardment may be expected to last 1 hour and will commence at 8-30 p.m. (3-30 p.m.)

4. O.C. Right Sub-Sector will clear trenches D.4, D.5, D.6. leaving L.Gun in D.4.Bay 3, D.6,Bays 3 & 18. Support trenches behind D 5 will not be occupied. Trenches to be clear by 3-15 p.m.

5. The 57th T.M.Battery will co-operate and fire up to 100 rounds.

6. O.C.Right Sub-Sector will be notified when the trenches may be occupied again.

7. Correct time will be given at 2 p.m. by telephone.

                                    (sd) R.A.Bulloch,Major.

Brigade Order, 16th August 1916. Author's collection.

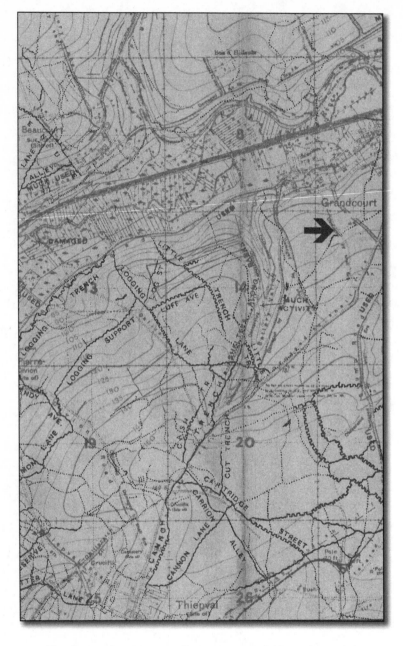

Trench map showing area of operations, 18th November 1916.
Arrow marks the approximate location in "Wretched Tea Trench" where Charles
Lander was wounded. Author's collection.

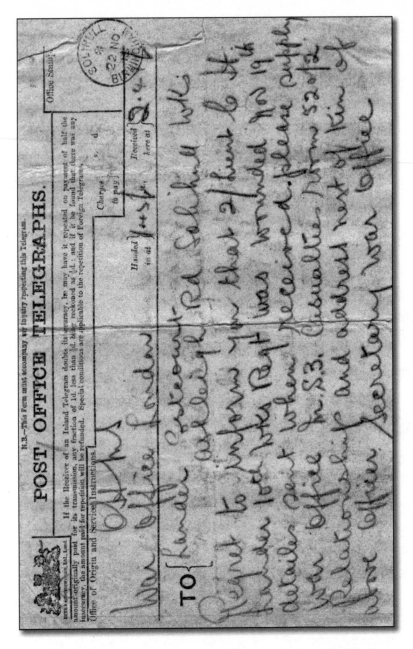

Telegram, 22nd November, 1916. Detailing injury sustained by Charles.
Author's collection.

1917

Soldiers having tea, Messines, Belgium, 1917.
Trustees of the National Library of Scotland.

January 9th

Reported to reserve battalion at Parkhurst Barracks, Isle of Wight. At this time of the year and at the period of the war, reserve battalions were not very cheery places and the ten days spent here were most boring. There was a pig of an adjutant (Capt. Archdeacon) nicknamed by the ranks "arch-dunghole". He was a singer by profession and had never been out and never did go out. The place seemed full of dugout Majors, the type who went sick when there was anything doing; and drank and played bridge all day. The younger members of the mess were therefore in the way and soon got drafted out again.

❖

January 20th

Received orders to report to Command Depot Ballyvonear, Co. Cork, Ireland. The lads told me it was the last place God made and that I should stay here and rot, forgotten until the end of the war.

❖

January 21st

Anyway I was glad to get away from Parkhurst and left the Isle of Wight on the morning of 21/1/17, crossing to Ireland on the night boat by way of Fishguard – Rosslare. A good crossing but my sleep was much disturbed by the movement of the rudder chains as the ship continually changed her course owing to the submarine menace. Also to me a far more disturbing feature of the journey was that my kit bag had vanished from the van somewhere between Bristol and Fishguard. The lovely early morning journey to Buttevant was completely spoilt by the haunting fear that I had lost my precious kit bag. All I had with me was a haversack with shaving tackle and some grub. I arrived at Buttevant about 10am and was directed to the camp, which was some miles north at the foot of the Ballyhouse mountains.

❖

January 22nd

I mounted a jaunty car and proceeded through the village of Buttevant which seemed strangely peaceful. The inhabitants who seemed to be just wasting their time, glared at us and occasionally spat and I began to realise that I was now in a hostile country. The driver smiled and was chatty and respectful though his language was quite foreign to me. We pulled up at the camp and I settled my account with the driver. Of course he robbed me, but this I didn't discover till later. I reported and was allotted quarters – a room to myself all nice and comfortable. Life for the next four months was much appreciated by me, though this peaceful life didn't suit the majority of subalterns. The C.O. was a most considerate old chap, back to duty from the retired list. There were about 500 other ranks in camp all in varying stages of convalescence and our job was to make them fit again for the slaughter.

About ten days later my kit arrived having been thrown out at some wayside station where it had lain until, strange to say, seen by another officer of the same name who took the trouble to inform me through my bankers.

I soon dropped in for a good job being given command of the training company. The object of this company was to finally test the men's fitness before they were returned to their units. The results being obtained chiefly by plenty of stiff company drill and long route marches. Any man falling by the wayside being returned for further treatment, due care being taken to stop malingering; but there was little of this as most men were thoroughly fed up with being in this wilderness, there being no women or other amusements.

While here it fell to my lot to conduct a number of drafts to Catterick Camp (Northern Command). I made great use of these opportunities to wangle a night or a weekend at home on my way back. After several medical boards, I was eventually marked fit and received orders again for overseas.

———— ❖ ————

May 12th

With many regrets I left Ballyvonear at 1pm on 12/5/17 and crossed to England by the night boat from Rosslare to Fishguard and arrived home 7.30pm.

———— ❖ ————

May 13th

Only three days at home and then to Southampton, reporting to R.T.O. at 2.30pm.

———— ❖ ————

May 17th

We left Southampton about 6.30pm on the Archangel. The ship waited off Spit Head until nightfall, then, being joined by a number of other transports, we were convoyed to Havre arriving early on the morning of 18/5/17. Here the troops were transferred to the St Taduo and we left Le Havre about 8.30am and proceeded slowly up the Seine to Rouen arriving about 2.30pm. A really glorious trip, spoilt by thoughts of home and the terrors of the future. I reported with others at the 19th Infantry Base Depot staying here until 4pm 23/5/17 and going through the usual gas drill and P.T. on the Bull ring during our stay here. After the usual tedious train journey lasting over 24 hours (Amiens, Abbeville, Etaples, Boulogne, Calais, St Omer and Hazebrouck) I detrained at Bailleul and walked to transport lines at Locre arriving at about 7pm on the 24/5/17 and reported to the Q.M. Lt Rossiter. Rations had gone up to the battalion so I was left in peace for one night at transport.

❖

May 25th

The next morning I joined the battalion in the line before Bois Quarante with Battalion H.Q. at Old Farm map ref N6 C 88. Lt-Col. RM Heath, D.S.O. still in command.

I was appointed to "C" Company (Capt. Westwood) then in support trenches. The situation was peaceful – for us. But the poor Boche was suffering and had been for some time; the whole of the ridge (Messines–Wytschaete) which he held, was all churned up: all brown, not a vestige of green anywhere as far as we could see. We spent the afternoon looking over toward the Boche lines and watching our artillery fire, though only a few hundred yards from his front line it was quite safe to raise our heads above the trenches in our support line. Our trenches were in good condition, though shallow on account of the water. They were revetted in the fire bays and all trenches boarded and with baby elephant shelters built into the trenches for our dugouts – small affairs big enough only to cover two or three men lying almost flat, but no cover from fire had the Boche retaliated. All the sump holes were infested with rats as big as rabbits waiting to devour the dead or even the dying.

There was something in the air but as yet t'was only a rumour, no orders having being given about the great attack on 7th June.

That evening the battalion was withdrawn from the front line and placed in brigade reserve in Ridge Wood occupying large shelters made of corrugated iron with many thicknesses of sand bags covering them.

❖

May 26th

We lay low during daylight and worked at night. The situation was quiet except for occasional short sharp bursts of artillery fire which made all scuttle for cover like rabbits. One of these strafes, more serious than the others, occurred one evening when a company was parading behind the wood taking up picks and shovels for a working party and causing the loss of one officer who was standing at the entrance to his dugout watching the proceedings. The situation became so disturbing that the whole battalion manned the reserve trenches and stood to. The shelling extended, and along the whole front there was a wonderful display of fireworks and M.G. bullets were flying about in all directions. Whether the Boche was making a raid or just jumpy, we never found out.

❖

May 28th

On the evening of 28/5/17 it fell to my lot to take charge of one of the working parties which consisted of preparing assembly positions on the banks of the Wytschaete beek in front of the Bois Carré. We made flats on the banks upon which we laid trench boards, camouflaging them as well as possible with grass and dirt; presumably these boards were used by the attacking infantry on the night of 6th and 7th June. The misgivings I had had when ordered to take this party did not materialise as we were left quite undisturbed and suffered no losses. When I arrived back at the company in the early morning I found that I had really been the lucky one, as they in the Ridge Wood position had been shelled all night.

❖

May 29th

We were relieved and marched back some seven miles to a hutment camp south of Westoutre. Here we spent the next week polishing up with the usual inspections. The chief item of interest while here was the watching from the top of Mt Rouge of a practice barrage by our artillery, on the Wytschaete–Messines Ridge; under cover of which some three companies made a great raid. They took about 150 prisoners and came back after messing up the German trenches. One of the objects of this daylight raid was to have the barrage photographed from the air so that the gunners could rectify any errors in range.

———— ❖ ————

June 5th

On the 5/6/17, orders were issued that the morrow was to be "Y" day. This meant the usual flood of last letters home which were deposited as usual with the Q.M. but fortunately only one had to be posted.

———— ❖ ————

June 6th "Y" Day

The battalion moved out of camp in fighting order during the morning and rested until dusk in a field a few hundred yards west of La Clytte. Here a good meal was provided from our cookers; bombs were issued and extra S.A.A. and flares.

My own job was 'O.C.' carrying party and while here my men reported and were issued with the material we had been ordered to carry. We were supplied with Yukon packs upon which we strapped the material. Although we had listened to a lecture on the use of these packs given by an old gold digger we experienced great difficulty in making the damn things comfortable and they were cursed plenty. They were not very satisfactory for the type of material we had to carry and were later discarded, the men preferring to carry in their hands; they felt more free and could take cover quicker. My party of 50 paraded about 7pm and moved off in file: a comical looking crowd with these heavily laden packs of war material; with rifles slung and stout sticks to help them along. Even Lt-Col. Heath couldn't refrain from smiling as I gave "eyes right" on passing out of the camp.

My carrying party had no difficulty in getting into position at the north-west corner of the Bois Carré N 12a 7.9 as orders had been issued that no wheeled transport was to be on the roads after 6pm "Y" day. The battalion had the same experience. A lesson well learnt from the failures of earlier attacks in the war, when the assembling infantry had been held up by traffic jams, only to arrive at their places worn out with cursing and the exertion of manoeuvring their heavily laden bodies passed artillery limbers G.S. wagons etc., and then only to arrive too late.

The battalion sergeant-major helped me to get the men settled in some discarded dugouts and trenches just inside the wood, with their packs all laid out ready. We then reconnoitred once again the best way to our front line, explained once again the situation to the other N.C.Os. and then settled down to a cup of tea. We couldn't sleep; we were all restless and we kept bobbing in and out of the dugout as different units came past to take up their positions. It was a still fine night, and all the troops seemed to us to move with uncanny silence. There was of course the usual intermittent artillery fire from our guns to keep the Boche from suspecting and to help cover any noise made by the tanks; overhead a few of our aeroplanes were flying low, watching.

Our own battalion passed; Maj. Fitzgerald in command, Lt-Col. Heath going to advanced brigade H.Q., situated in the mine shaft in Bois Carré. The 10th R Wks R H.Q., before going over, were at strong point 7 approx 0 7a 1.8 with the companies distributed along the Wytschaete beek to the right.

In good time I sent my report to battalion H.Q. that my party was in position and all OK. It has always seemed to me a masterly piece of work, this getting into position of something like 100,000 troops between the hours of dusk and dawn, and in time to get the OK back to the higher command; all accomplished in less than six hours. All credit must be given to Gen. Plumer (Second Army) and his Chief of Staff, Gen. Harrington.

❖

June 7th "Z" Day

It was still dark when at 3.10am the earth shook with the explosion of nineteen great mines and all our guns opened up a terrific fire, the field guns making the creeping barrage and the heavier stuff dealing with the enemy guns, strong points, cross roads etc.

We waited in suspense for the German reply. It was not long in coming. There was a terrific roar as a huge shell came roaring through the wood and buried itself on the north-west edge within 30x of our abode, a momentary pause, and a terrific explosion which put out our lights and almost buried us in debris. We had scarce time to relight our candles when over came another of the same quality, this time a little nearer. We said our prayers, for had the Boche continued to traverse left the next one would have blotted us out. We waited for some time hugging the ground but strange to say no more came our way and at last we ventured out to have a look round. The holes these two shells had made were the biggest I had ever seen quite 10 yards across and 10 foot deep and the nearest was no more than 20x from us. The Germans evidently thought that they would catch our infantry assembling behind the wood; it certainly was a likely place but all our infantry were well forward. About 30 minutes after zero German prisoners carrying nothing but their gas bag tins began to trickle past our post. The usual smug-faced lot, they smiled at us poor devils waiting to go into it. We learnt that the German front and support lines were now in our hands. This being all the information we could get, we waited until zero + 3hrs 10. My carrying party of 25 moved off leaving the remaining 25 behind under the battalion sergeant-major as arranged. Proceeding along the south edge of the Bois Carré we came up behind our own battalion at about zero + 3.30hrs as it was preparing to leave the old German support line. This line and the old German front line were now being held in strength by the brigade that went over to the assault at zero hour. There was precious little left of these trenches and very few dead about, the Germans evidently not having held them in strength. I do remember seeing half a dozen fat corpses, probably a German M.G. crew who had stuck it and got laid out. Against these enemy losses I came across a few of our own dead at the bottom of a sap between our old front and German front lines; most likely they had been placed here by the order of some officer in case the sight of them might affect the morale of troops going over later.

Leaving the old German support line behind our battalion, about zero + 4.0hrs, we moved slowly forward; we hadn't much time to look round but even so we soon lost touch with our battalion in the mist of battle. I had great difficulty in maintaining direction as landmarks were few, the only guide being the north-west edge of the Grand Bois. Halting again at zero + 4.30 (behind the Green Line) for a few moments to get my party into some order again we then advanced at zero + 4.45 behind the most intensive barrage to the final assault, our battalion being now in extended order. Although we were less than 100x behind the rear wave it was quite impossible to see anything of the assault, our artillery barrage appeared to us just one vast wall of smoke and flame enveloping all.

We now met our first real trouble; shells fell thick among us, completely scattering my heavily laden party. They seemed to melt into the ground and all seemed lost and I saw myself arriving at H.Q. without the goods. The shelling suddenly ceased and my carrying party as suddenly re-appeared, complete to a man; they had only taken cover. Hastily pushing on we soon came up to the battalion. Here we dumped the goods and reported to battalion H.Q. at zero + 5.10. The companies were busy digging in, under cover of an outpost company who moved forward still under cover of our barrage, and took up a position on the east side of Oosttavern Wood.

There had been few casualties and all were merry and bright. Prisoners were being formed up and marched back by the score including a number of German officers (we having captured, just behind the Black Line, a German regimental H.Q.). There were very few German casualties; their Black Line had not been flattened out like their front and support lines and so they had been able to get cover from our shrapnel barrage, hugging the bottom of their trench until our men were upon them. They seemed pretty scared and glad to be out of it. Their officers were a bit saucy though and one big bug demanded an officer escort, so we sent him down in the charge of one of the most disreputable looking privates in the battalion; 'Tommy' took his badges as souvenirs and put his prisoner in the corps cage for other ranks; here he spit and spluttered for hours before he could make himself understood and get transferred to the officers' quarters. He was a regimental commander.

Before returning with my party, now laden with German machine guns, periscopes and other trophies, to the Bois Carré I had a few minutes to look round, and visited "D" Company officers recalling to them our toast of the previous "Y" day. A toast to our next meeting at the Black Line. The most optimistic of us then never expected that all four of us would reach our objective.

The German gunners were now intent on saving their guns as by now our outpost line was almost upon them; we were left in peace to consolidate our gains while our aeroplanes were busy overhead, up and down the line, plotting our position as marked by flares and answering our signals (sent on ground signalling panel) with their klaxon horns. This was dangerous work for the R.F.C. and I saw two of our planes float down in pieces having being hit by our own shells. Our only casualty while I was with the battalion was caused by a falling shell case which smashed a man's leg to pulp. The aeroplanes to be safe from our shell fire, should have flown at a height which would keep them between the trajectory of our field guns and of our Howitzers but if they couldn't get our signals they came lower and risked it.

We arrived back at the Bois Carré about 11 am and had a meal and sent up the other half of our party under the sergeant-major and a guide with a further supply of wire and bombs etc. During the afternoon I received orders from brigade to proceed with all my carrying party to the battalion in the line, each man taking 4 gallons of water (two petrol tins). We followed a new track which had been taped out by the Divisional scouts. When we came near the Black Line once again we got badly shelled but luck was with us and we escaped without loss. Arriving at the position held by the battalion in the morning we discovered that the whole of the 57th Brigade had again moved forward and the Black Line trenches were now held in strength by other troops in support. Our own battalion was somewhere in front, so leaving my party under cover I proceeded to make a reconnaissance taking with me the sergeant-major and a couple of runners. Passing through the wood and on to the village of Oosttaverne we came into contact with one of our companies forming up and having a roll-call; each company was being withdrawn from the line in turn for this purpose. Battalion H.Q. were in a shell hole covered by a hedge just south of the Oosttaverne–Hollebeke Road (0 21b 9.8). The water was handed over and distributed to the thirsty troops. Although it was still daylight it was quite possible to move about as our guns were still putting down a good barrage; which was in response to an S.O.S. some time previously when German infantry had made some shew at forming for a counter attack. The battalion suffered some casualties at this time as our barrage was short (or we had gone too far) and we had to withdraw our line a little. Considering that all our field guns had moved forward during the day, their positions now being about our old front line, this evening barrage was more wonderful than had been that of zero hour. These new positions (Odonto Line) had been taken up at zero +12 hours; the C.O. only having about half an hour in which to call his company commanders together and make his preparations for this advance. The original orders being that another division was to come up and move through us; but owing to the complete success of our morning's work and our insignificant losses we were thought capable of this further effort; and so we were, the new division still being kept in reserve.

My carrying party returned to the Bois Carré for the night. On the way back we took things easy and had a good look round for souvenirs in the concrete dugouts of Oosttaverne Wood; many of these were palatial places, the largest having been already turned into an aid post.

There was a battery of German 77mm along a hedge north-west of Oosttaverne which our battalion had taken in the advance. Numerous guns and limbers with many dead horses littered the Verne Road (from village of

Oosttaverne S.W. to 0.21 central). The German gunners must have had a very unhealthy time trying to save their guns in our merciless barrage. The most forward German battery that we noticed had been on the eastern edge of Croonaert Wood in the line of advance of the battalion on our right; it was all blown to pieces as also were the shelters for its gunners and had probably been destroyed some days before.

❖

June 8th

The following day we carried up a further supply of stores and got heavily shelled with black H.E. shrapnel as we proceeded in file along the St Elois-Oosttaverne Road about 0 15c 9.4. This road which was on top of the ridge was probably in full view of the German O.P.'s (Observation Posts) in Green Wood. I got a piece in the face and Cpl Cheshire a good one in the knee with which he bolted to the dressing station. I had to carry on to battalion H.Q. which was still in a shell hole at 0 21b 9.8. On the way back to Bois Carré where we spent another night, I called at an aid post to get inoculated as a precaution though the wound was only slight and this was how I got into the casualty list for the second time.

❖

June 9th

During the day the 10th R Wks R was relieved from its position in the front line and came back into brigade reserve, in the Black Line east of Croonaert Wood where Lt-Col. R.M. Heath took over the command with H.Q. in a concrete pill box about 0 14c 6.8.

❖

June 10th

We were all relieved in the evening and marched to a hutment camp at Canada Corner, Locre, arriving about 9.30pm, and being played into camp by the division band to the tune of "Here the conquering Heroes come" and felt very proud of ourselves.

The great success of the 7th of June was primarily due to the infinite pains taken by the staff of Gen. Plumer's Second Army (Gen. Harrington, Chief of Staff) to work out every detail.
The chief ones being:

- *Good jumping off places for the great concentration of infantry and arrangements for a slow methodical advance under a perfect barrage (artillery concentration approx one gun to every 10 yards);*
- *The shattering effect of our mines (nineteen) on the morale of the German forward troops;*
- *Accurate large maps prepared from aerial reconnaissance and other means which were supplied to all junior officers;*
- *Forward supply of stores;*
- *Effective contact with R.A.F. (R.F.C.) after objective taken;*
- *Removal of all wheeled transport from our roads after 6pm on "Y" day; and*
- *Fine weather and dry ground.*

Four clear days were spent at Canada Corner resting and cleaning up.

———————— ❖ ————————

June 15th

On 15/6/17 we moved up again in brigade reserve to positions south-east of Oosttaverne Wood; my company "C" (Capt. Westwood) posted in a bit of trench about 0 20b 6.7 with battalion H.Q. in a concrete pill box in Leg Copse. We moved off for this relief rather early, it being still daylight as we topped the Vierstraat ridge and came in full view of the German sausage balloons. It was asking for trouble and we got it when nearing the south-west edge of Oosttaverne Wood. The Germans calculating accurately the time we should take to reach here dropped a couple of 8-inch shells among us, knocking out a dozen of us (two killed) and burying as many more; I myself was knocked completely over by the force of one of the explosions.

The only items of interest apart from food as we lay in these trenches for three days was the great aerial activity displayed by both sides. The Germans were really on top as Baron von Richthofen's flying circus was in this area, being drawn here no doubt by the 7th June attack and the preparations now being made for the 3rd Battle of Ypres (31/7/17). We saw a number of battles in the air and one of our planes catch fire quite low overhead: a terrible sight. We learned later though, that this plane had made a safe landing in our lines and that the hair of the pilot had turned grey through his ordeal. Of more humorous interest was the CO's daily bath in a shell hole and his afternoon siesta in his deckchair complete with cigar.

June 18th

Orders arrived for us to relieve the front line. I was feeling pretty seedy and getting the wind up, so went to see the M.O. (Dr Covington) in his aid post, a huge concrete building in Oosttaverne Wood. I had a high temperature and pulse so got sent down with the other wounded to the A.D.S at Locre; examined again, I was put on a stretcher nicely tucked up in blankets and sent to No. 2 C.C.S. at Bailleul arriving after 11pm and spent a glorious night between clean sheets once more.

June 19th

The following afternoon I was cleared to No. 7 Stationary Hospital (by train from Bailleul station) arriving in the small hours of the morning.

June 20th

Here I spent a week in bed while my temperature returned to normal all too quickly. A couple of days dressed and about enabled me to look around this ancient town and docks and to visit the fishing village of La Portel and the resort of Wimereaux.

June 29th

Passed for light duty at the base and left by passenger train for Rouen, reporting to the Cyclists' base depot where I stayed for another two weeks' holiday.

July 17th

Received movement orders and left Rouen by troop train 4pm and after travelling at the usual speed via Amiens, Abbeville, Boulogne, Calais and Hazebrouck detrained at Bailleul 28 hours later and reported to the Q.M. (Rossiter) at transport line near Hyde Park Corner, Locre.

❖

July 19th

Spent the night at transport and reported to battalion H.Q. in a field about N 22 C the following morning and got posted to "C" Company (Capt. Westwood). The other officers of the company being Bostick and Brazier. Three nights were spent here in bivouac, most of the time being spent on working parties cleaning up the newly captured ground, collecting old arms, ammunition, shell cases, clothing etc., in fact any old rubbish, which was put into dumps to be taken to the base. This was an economy stunt engineered from home; quite necessary no doubt but very irksome to the troops who knew that munition workers at home were making anything from £10 to £20 per week and threatening all the time to strike for more. I clicked for two of these working parties and got shelled most of the time as we were always under observation from sausage balloons; though my parties suffered no casualties it was very jumpy work and more risky than being in the front line.

While here I received my promotion to lieutenant and put up my second star; this promotion was general for all second lieutenants of two years standing; provided of course that no adverse reports had been sent in about them. The promotions were ante-dated so that I had credited to me an extra £6 pay. I was saving money quite fast while on active service as there was nothing to spend it on. My pay now was 1/6 and 2/6 a day field allowance plus the usual army rations, while my mess bills were only about 50fr a week (27fr to £1)

❖

July 22nd

At about 3.30pm the battalion moved forward again, this time to a sector still further north. "C" Company being in support behind Ravine Wood 0

10a 3.6 with battalion H.Q. in a shack in Denys Wood 0 9 d. The relief was completed in daylight, moving in small parties by way of our old front line and the Daum Strasse. "C" Company H.Q. was also in a shack providing cover from view only. It was at any rate spacious and dry and fortunately the Boche artillery paid little attention to this quarter. Most of the German shell fire seemed to be concentrated on Delbske Farm and on Ravine Wood, particularly to a concrete dugout in the sunken road where F.P. Smith had his "D" Company H.Q. The place was so strong that 5.9 bounced off it.

There was much interest taken every morning at a German plane which came over at dawn flying very low, so we took good care not to expose our H.Q. and left him for other people to strafe,so he always got off unscathed.

❖

July 25th

In the evening I had to take a large working party to construct a communication trench from Rose Wood to our front line near cross roads about 200x N.W. of Green Wood under supervision of the Royal Engineers. We got shelled by gas on the way; just enough to make the boys jumpy but when actually on the job were left in peace.

On June 7th the front line was along the eastern edge of Rose Wood to Verhaest Farm; later when I was comfortable at the base, the 10th R Wks R had the job of pushing the front line forward to Green Wood. It was a night operation and we lost Lt Bernard, severely wounded, and a number of other good men. We took a German patrol, but why on earth the forward line was not taken up on June 7th when there was no opposition, Lord only knows!

❖

July 26th

I had to take over a section of the front line about 0 11c 3.3 with most of "C" Company. Both sides were still very jumpy and as for some time past scarcely a night passed without an S.O.S. going up. Somewhere to our right (our S.O.S. was red over green over yellow) and the guns of both sides would all open up and we were treated to a wonderful display of fireworks as we all stood to, waiting and watching.

There was a particularly hot spot on our right about 0 17c 1.1 (junction buildings) which changed hands almost every night and sometimes twice nightly; it was pretty easy to take but for some reason just as easy to lose and this caused most of the trouble. Fortunately the 10th R Wks R was never called upon to take it.

———————— ❖ ————————

July 27th

The battalion sent out a strong fighting patrol in front of my sector under 2nd-Lt Durety; although elaborate arrangements had been made whatever they were looking for they didn't find and returned without a scalp.

It was about this time that we experienced a real strafe from the German gas shells. Like most things new, these shells caused casualties, particularly affecting the eyes and lungs; and as they were usually put over mixed with H.E. shells their presence was at first not noticed as they burst on percussion with very little noise and had no smell. Should any of the vapour from these shells touch the skin, great blisters full of water came up and a couple of good sniffs were a sure case for Blighty while a particle in the eyes meant blindness, often permanent. I have seen as many as a dozen men being led back blind, many for life. This was Germany's latest and worst form of frightfulness.

———————— ❖ ————————

July 28th

There was a very heavy strafe of our front lines and Ravine Wood; the company on my left suffering very heavy casualties; though for some reason my bit of line remained untouched in spite of the fact that it was dug through some farm buildings and its right rested on cross roads. After the strafe was over and the stretcher bearers were doing their best to clear the wounded I went over to the left to see F.P. Smith as it was his 21st birthday but he had had a dose of gas and was on the way home.

———————— ❖ ————————

July 29th

This was my 24th birthday, the second I had spent in hell. Tonight the battalion was relieved and went back for one day to bivouac at Butterfly Farm N.19a 6.9 arriving about 4am 30/7/17. It was a ridiculously long way back for so short a time, as the battalion had to go up again that night to take part in the great battle of 31/7/17 (3rd Ypres). There was cheery news awaiting me this night as I was ordered to report to the 9th Corps school at Berthen, at which place I reported about 7.30pm on 30/7/17. This school was a general course for subalterns and lasted 4 weeks. The grub was really rotten and arrangements for work none too good. As I didn't see eye to eye with the platoon commander, it received a poor report in consequence. While on this course the battalion had been back to west of St Omer for a rest and refit, which included a visit to the seaside for one day.

❖

August 26th

I left Berthen at 6am and entrained at Bailleul for St Omer; arriving 3.30pm same day and on reporting to the town Mayor was billeted in the town for one night.

❖

August 27th

Next day I took the train to Ebbinghem and marched a couple of kilometres north to Le Nieppe (Trois Rois) where I got in touch with my battalion again when they debussed and billeted there for the night on their way back to the line. Next day the battalion marched via Bavinchove and Hondeghem to billets at Rouge Croix 2km west of Fletre arriving about 4pm.

We spent a pleasant week here doing a few parades in the morning and a little map reading for young officers in the afternoon.

It was here one evening while going home to roost, another officer and myself were literally chased by a Boche plane dropping bombs. We ran for cover of some farm buildings, thereby increasing the target, instead of just dropping down in the nearest ditch.

While here I explored the ground round Meteren, the scene of a fight in the early days of the war by our 1st Battalion who were pushing back the Boche during the race for the coast. The graves of the fallen, all well tended, were scattered about the low ground to the south of Meteren.

❖

September 29th

The battalion marched via Meteren to camp (tents) on the western slopes of Mt Vidaigne. That night I received orders to proceed next day to 9th Corps Signal School on Mt Noir for a six-week course, which course I did not finish as I was recalled by telegram to take the place of Lt C.C. Hatwood (battalion signals officer) who had been wounded.

❖

September 30th

I rejoined the battalion in reserve at Kemmel Shelters N 19c 8.1 about midday.

❖

October 11th

The battalion moved up to trenches in front of Klein Zillebeke with battalion H.Q. in concrete pill box in 1.36c 3.8 Fusilier Wood, our way up being passed the Spoil Bank (brigade H.Q.) and Transport Corner. The road was very congested with transport, particularly lorries laden with heavy shells.

During my absence from the battalion they had been engaged in the 3rd Battle of Ypres. The shew itself as far as our battalion and the 57th Brigade were concerned had been a complete success; our chief losses had occurred while in the assembly positions about Transport Corner where we lost Lts Bostock and Brazier killed. The Germans really lost heavily, as apart from their losses in the initial attack; they had been caught de-bussing at Zandvoorde by our heavies as they prepared to counter attack. The information about this counter attack had been got back in time by pigeon post and also by telephone as strange to say, our line was through to brigade at the critical moment; for this piece of work the brigade signal officer (Lt Burnette) received the M.C.

Battalion Sgt Major Pratt was killed in this action; he was a huge heavy man, a dear good natured soul loved by everybody. He was badly hit in the side near Klein Zillebeke and refused aid from our stretcher bearers, walking all the way back to the dressing station near the Spoil Bank where he collapsed and died. It was about this time that our divisional general, Tom Bridges, stopped one in the leg when near his battle H.Q. at the Spoil Bank. When he arrived at the A.D.S. at Locre and was told he would have to lose his leg, he said "give it to the lion" (divisional mascot). When convalescent Gen. Bridges was sent on a mission to the U.S.A. and after the war was given the Governor Generalship of one of the Australian provinces.

Brig.-Gen. Jeffreys who had been in command of the 57th Infantry Brigade on the Somme now took over command of the division. Gen. Cubitt was now in command of 57th Infantry Brigade. He had been a gunner and like most men who had had a lot to do with horses was a great linguist. It is on record that one night as our men were being relieved and not yet out of the forward area, they saw someone smoking and shouted 'put that B---- light out.' The answer came back 'who the B---- H-- are you ?' Our men shouted 'The B---- Warwicks,' to which the smoker replied 'And I'm your B--- General.'

After the war Maj. Brindley saw Gen. Cubitt and after congratulating him on his appointment as Governor General of the Bermudas, asked him if he knew any Bermudan swear words. "No", said General Cubitt, "but they'll B--- soon know some of mine".

The Fusilier Wood Battalion H.Q. was in an old German concrete shelter, very small and dirty,so I had to find quarters in a nearby shelter with some machine gunners so Col. Heath would have plenty of breathing space for himself. These H.Qs had cover from view being in a hollow near the railway and we were left in peace. I did not have to go into the front line and apart from my signal job there was little to do. One nasty job fell to my lot: that of going back along the duck board track one pouring wet night to meet a working party at Transport Corner, a windy job as there was no cover all the way. I was out of luck this trip as, when trying to fix up visual communication with advanced brigade H.Q. at the Bluff (0 4b 5.7), I forgot to subtract the magnetic variation from my bearings and so failed. Col. Heath smiled sarcastically.

--- ❖ ---

October 14th

The battalion was relieved on 14/10/17 and went into brigade reserve in tunnels at Hill 60 and Larch Wood. Through some mistake I had to trek all the way back to transport at Siege Farm and took a route along the canal bank past Lock No. 6.

--- ❖ ---

October 15th

In the morning I returned to battalion H.Q. at Hill 60 and had a rotten passage up the Verbrandenmolen Road, having to put my skates on as the Boche was shelling heavily all the time, so arrived breathless and a little scared, to the amusement of all. We spent two nights here in the bowels of the earth, only going out for my own amusement to inspect the remains of Hill 60 which had earned such a name for itself earlier in the war.

❖

October 17th

On the evening of 17/10/17 the battalion took over another sector of the brigade front in Shrewsbury Forest with battalion H.Q. in spacious concrete pill boxes at Image Crescent (C 25c 9.3). The relief was completed without casualties, though it was a nasty stretch of open country we had to traverse past Corner House where the battalion left our company in reserve; to which company I had to lay a telephone line which was always going fut; so I gave it up and went to bed. This was a great mistake as the C.O. found out he was not in communication with the reserve company; he fetched me out in the small hours and ticked me off. This slackness on my part might have lost the war judging by the C.O.'s wrath.

❖

October 19th

On the evening of the 19/10/17 the battalion was relieved after a comparatively peaceful time in Bulgar Wood. I went back to transport at Siege Farm and the battalion bivouacked in a field near Beggars Rest (N d 2.8). The conditions were appalling, the weather now being very bad; wet and cold and the men only having their ground sheets with which to provide cover. Some very ingenious shelters were made with the aid of a few sticks and these ground sheets, into which the men crawled in twos and fours. At transport lines, I shared a tent with Padre Rocliffe (R.C.) and messed with Rossiter (Q.M.), 2nd-Lt Durety (Intelligence Officer) and 2nd-Lt Rockford (Transport). Our nights were very disturbed by enemy bombing and I thoroughly got the wind up; being far more uncomfortable than when in action. The padre slept soundly through it all; he trusted in the Lord. The battalion suffered several casualties through enemy bombs. One bomb of heavy delayed action type, dropped by the side of a tent in which fourteen men were sleeping and blew it to shreds yet hurting no one in the tent but causing casualties among officers and men at least 100 yards away.

❖

November 4th

On the 4/11/17 the battalion again moved forward to the tunnels of Hill 60 and Larch Wood and did two more days in the line in front of Shrewsbury Forest.

The brigade was withdrawn from action on the night of 9/11/17 and after spending one night in bivouac at Beggars Rest were taken back by motor lorries to the Meteren area; arriving at billets there about 3.30pm on 10/11/17. Here we were all set to clean up and fatten up.

❖

November 12th

The battalion entrained at Caestre and went into billets at Belle Croix (½ km south of Wardrecques) detraining at Ebblinghem. Here we continued our clearing up and doing company training in preparation for an inspection. Sports and competitions were also held while stationed here. Many new officers and drafts arrived and we all had our photos taken to send home to mother. We were now in civilisation and enjoying life once again, especially as leave had started once again and I was near the top of the list. I kept a keen eye on that list in the orderly room, battalion H.Q. being in a chateau near Wardrecques station.

❖

November 26th

The battalion marched via the canal bank, Arques and St Martin-au-Laert to a rifle range near Tilques about 5km north west of St Omer where we spent two most uncomfortable nights in tents, very crowded and very wet and cold as it was snowing most of the time and there was no facility for cooking.

❖

November 28th

We returned by the same route to Belle Croix and on 30/11/17 I was given my ticket to Blighty for fourteen days leave of absence.

❖

December 1st

I left Belle Croix about 11am on 1/12/17 a few hours before my leave was due; but I didn't like the idea of getting up in the middle of the night to catch a train. Besides, I might have overslept, so decided to foot it to Calais. I got a lift by car as far as St Omer and after walking some little way along the Calais Road, picked up with some A.S.C. men in a lorry and was driven all the way to Calais via Ardres without another change. After reporting at the quay to the embarkation officer to enquire as to the time of the boat, I went into the old town and fixed up at the officers' club for the night.

❖

December 2nd

Left Calais 12.45pm for Dover. Leave train waiting on quay; sent a telegram home and entered restaurant car where special lunch was ready. What a meal – a good honest steak with chips and beer. I never before appreciated a meal or life so much as I did that afternoon.

❖

December 3rd

Arrived in Birmingham about 12 midnight and went to 15, Clarendon Road being too late for Solihull. These two weeks came all too quickly to an end.

❖

December 14th

On the morning of 14/12/17 I started my journey back to the line. I spent the night of 14/12/17 at Ruislip after going to see the Byng boys but even George Roby failed to make me smile, such was one's state of mind on returning from leave. The night of 15/12/17 had to be spent in the waiting room at Charing

Cross station as the leave train left at 8am and arrived at Dover about 11am, where I had lunch with F.P. Smith, before embarking for Calais. At which place I arrived about 5.30pm and had to spend an uncomfortable night somewhere in a tent, moving down by train to Etaples next day, 17/12/17 at 2pm. Arriving at Etaples at 6pm I fixed up (after reporting) at the Club and awaited orders.

❖

December 19th

Received movement orders on 19/12/17 and left Etaples by train at 7am.

❖

December 20th

Arrived at Rocquigny (rail head) in the desolate Somme area about 10pm same day having travelled via Abbeville and Amiens. With a few others returning from leave we spent the night in a lorry hut by the side of the railway, cold, hungry and generally fed up, waiting for dawn so that we could march on to our respective units. We were all expecting to get into another Somme battle as by now we all realised that our units were holding the line in front of Marcoing – the scene of the great surprise attack of November. As we approached our transport lines, we all expected to be greeted with the familiar words 'you're for it' but strange to say everyone was happy and we were told that some units had not had a casualty for a fortnight. 'The line is absolutely cushy,' they said. So different from what had been expected and from what we had left behind up north.

❖

December 21st

The transport lines of the 57th Brigade were at Neuville about 1km south-west of Havrincourt Wood. At the time of rejoining 21/12/17 the battalion was in bivouacs in Havrincourt Wood. I stayed at transport, as was usual when out of the line, and shared a tent in the shattered village of Neuville.

The 19th Division stayed another two months in this area before going back into corps reserve so that I became well acquainted with the district which had little to interest anyone, especially at this time of the year. The

Germans, when they retired to the Hindenburg Line, had systematically destroyed everything: even the fruit trees had been sawed down. Most of the troops in reserve were in bivouacs. H.Q.s and a few of the transport had bell tents, while a few enterprising men had rigged up lean-to shelters against bits of wall with their ground sheets. One enterprising pair of old sweats had found a pigsty which they had made into the best billet in the village; it was dry if not clean and offered protection against air bombs which caused us many a sleepless night.

———— ❖ ————

December 23rd

The battalion took over a sector of the newly captured Hindenburg Line in front of Marcoing, with its right flank in Coullet Wood and left at Ribecourt exclusive.

I was again with H.Q. as Signal Officer and earlier in the day had the job of reconnoitring the position. We relieved by daylight, marching by platoon, south of Havrincourt Wood to Mety and then along the Trescault Road which was well camouflaged, and entering the trenches our side of the ridge. There was no great concentration of troops or guns and little evidence of a great fight having taken place recently: the ground was frost-bound and hardly marked by shell fire, the trenches were dug deep in the chalky ground and trench-boarded and well revetted, with many fine deep dugouts in all sorts of odd places. Two companies were in front line and two in support (old Hindenburg support) with battalion H.Q. in dugout in support.

———— ❖ ————

December 25th

Christmas Day was spent in the line; all was quiet. The weather for some weeks now was frosty and ground covered in snow; we had a few men suffer from frostbite but other losses were negligible.

A certain amount of patrolling was undertaken at night, as the distance between the lines was very great. The Germans outpost line being on the outskirts of Marcoing, at night we held some old German gun pits about 500x in front of our line just to keep an eye on old Fritz's night work. We lost a good signaller from this post in unfortunate circumstances, as he was accidentally shot dead by one of our battalion scouts. One night 2nd-Lt

Durety was detailed to take out a patrol and called at this outpost to warn them of his movements. A few minutes after he had left the post the C.O. rang him up to say he wanted to speak to 2nd-Lt Durety and one of the signallers ran after him to give him the C.O.'s message. In the darkness the signaller was not recognised and after challenging him two or three times, to which he made no reply, one of the scouts fired at him, killing him instantly, shot in the head.

While we were holding this sector the Germans wearing white smocks came over the snow and attacked with liquid fire the battalion on our right, who were holding Welsh Ridge. They succeeded in penetrating to the support trenches but were driven out again by a counter attack later the same day. Fortunately the trouble didn't extend to our front. We made several tours of duty in this sector, going back to Havrincourt Wood for rest and clean.

We were bombed almost every night and the weather was perishing cold, so that real sleep was impossible. The division Follies gave their shew to the troops at rest, but although there was no other amusement the shew was poorly attended and the troupe had great difficulty in getting anything over. The spirit of the troops was sinking fast owing to the conditions, as by now the thaw had set in and quite one third of the battalion had trench feet or other conditions. Trench feet could be prevented by rubbing with whale oil and a frequent change of socks, and junior officers got all the blame for this type of casualty. During one of our spells out of the line I was lucky enough to get a night in Amiens. Going by lorry and train from rail head, but having no friend to go with (one officer per battalion per day) the treat fell rather flat. Though it was good to get into civilisation again even for one night.

❖

To all Coys. W.P.18/6.

The Support line working Party to-night is cancelled.

A Party of 1 Officer, C Coy. and 75 other ranks,

(B Coy. 34, C Coy. 41,) will report to Representative,

of 82nd.Fld.Coy.,R.E., at 9-30.P.M. to-night at the

point where POPPY LANE crosses WYTSCHAETEBEK,

(N.12.c.6½.5.) for work on WYTSCHAETEBEK.

One shovel per man will be carried.

(sd) W.H.Brindley.
Capt.&.Adjt.

28th.May,1917.

May 1917 Note from Capt. Brindley. Author's collection.

"A" Form.
MESSAGES AND SIGNALS.

Army Form C.2121
(In pads of 100.)
No. of Mess ge___

Prefix	Code	m.	Words	Charge	This message is on a/c of :	Recd. at___'___m
Office of Origin and Service Instructions.			Sent		Service.	Date___
			At___m.			From___
			To___			By___
			By		(Signature of " Franking Officer ")	

TO

| Sender's Number | Day of Month. | In reply to Number. | A A A |
| * **SC 75** | **5** | | |

Water 400 tins will be taken up
to night also YUKON PACKS Latter
should be at a Transport lines by 6
+ O.C. N° informed that they are to go
up with the water.
25 men + yourself must be at
BRASSERIE by 10 p.m. another dump
of 100 tins will be placed in BOIS CARRI
[...] N6c8½ Each of your own dumps
= 75. All will assist in building up new
dump. [...] material [...]
am asking for a lorry but don't rely
on it. Don't forget to take up a relief for
guard + take up the guards Tommies cookers to
[...]

From			
Place	**57' LD**		
Time			

| The above may be forwarded as now corrected. | (Z) | |
| Censor. | Signature of Addressor or person authorised to telegraph in his name |

(710;) Wt. W12093/M1217 50,000 pads. 1/17. D.D.&L. (E764) Form C/212;/11.

June 1917. Messages and Signals. Author's collection.

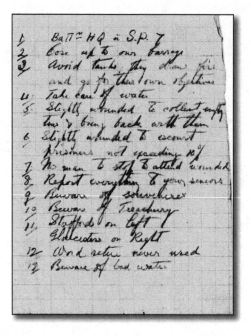

June 1917. Handwritten diary notes prior to the Battle of Messines.
Author's collection.

Charles Lander's handwritten notes transcribed from above page taken
following instructions for the Battle of Messines, June 7th 1917.

1   - *Battalion H.Q. in S.P. 7*
2   - *Close up to our barrage*
3   - *Avoid tanks, they draw fire and go for their own objective*
4   - *Take care of water*
5   - *Slightly wounded to collect empty tins (water) and bring back with them*
6   - *Slightly wounded to escort prisoners not exceeding 10%*
7   - *No man to stop to attend wounded*
8   - *Report everything to your seniors*
9   - *Beware of souvenirs*
10 - *Beware of Treachery (sic)*
11 - *Staffords on left Gloucester's on right*
12 - *Word retire never used*
13 - *Beware of bad water*

"At zero + 3hrs 10, my carrying party of 25 moved off leaving the remaining 25 behind under the Battalion Sgt Major as arranged. Proceeding along the south edge of the Bois Carre."

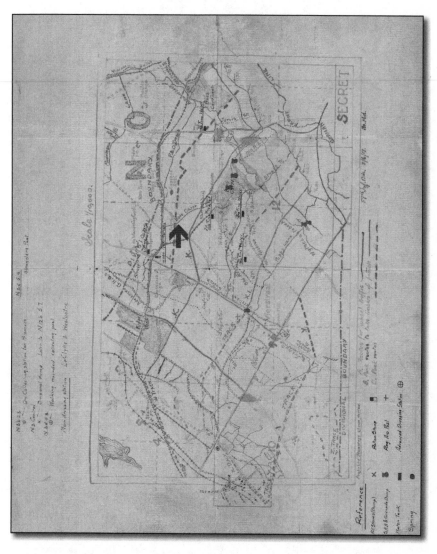

Map dated 3rd June 1917. Marked up by Charles Lander for the Battle of Messines. Map shows routes towards the German Front Line prior to the assault on 7th June. Author's collection.

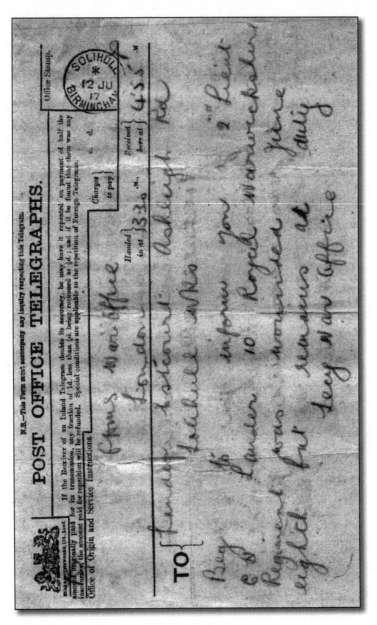

June 1917. Telegram notifying of Charles Lander's wounding.
Author's collection.

1918

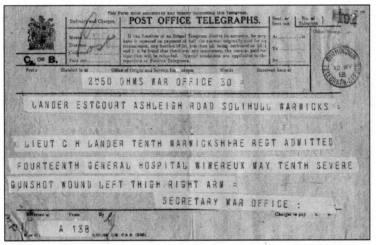

Telegram informing of Charles Lander's 3rd wounding.
Author's collection.

During February we switched over to the right of the brigade section on the railway and slopes of Welsh Ridge. The conditions were appalling in the trenches: knee deep in thick Somme mud. The Germans were even worse off and many times small parties were seen on top trying to make their positions more habitable. It was a case of live and let live until one day the brigadier came round and spied Jerry on top and he told us it wasn't war. After he had started us shooting he popped off to his cushy billet and left us to take cover from the retaliation. There were a number of derelict tanks on both ridges, relics of the November 1917 attack. One was in the German front line and they could be heard tinkering with this thing every night, but they never succeeded in getting it away.

An incident which caused much amusement to junior officers was a German who tried to give himself up and couldn't find anyone to surrender to until he got as far back as brigade H.Q. They must have thought the whole of the Third Army had given way, from the letter the C.O. received about the lack of vigilance on our front. Later it was proved that it was the front of the battalion on our right which this man had penetrated.

It was about this time that Lt-Col. Fitzgerald put up the D.S.O. This was in addition to the order of Leopold and Belgian Croix de Guerre which he had received for the Messines Ridge attack. Some folks have all the luck. I could never see that he did anything worthy of a decoration and I was with him at H.Q. all the time. The man who ran the shew on the 7th June as far as the 10th R Wks R was concerned was Maj. Martin (later given command of another battalion) who only got the M.C. But I suppose the man in command must get the credit as he would have had to take the blame if the battalion had failed.

───────── ❖ ─────────

February 18th

Battalion was relieved and after spending two nights in Neuville and Havrincourt Wood cleaning up, they marched back via Ytres and Rocquigny to huts at Beaulencourt on the Bapaume - Perrone Road, 20/2/18. The 19th Division was now in corps reserve and went into training in preparation for the expected German offensive which was to begin on March 21st.

While at rest here, apart from the usual training, we were practiced in moving forward to positions behind Hermies and Doignies. Presumably this was expected to be the danger spot as far as our Corps was concerned. A number of new trenches had been dug about this area but as they were only about two feet deep; very wide and not wired, they seemed pretty useless to me as they were all so obvious and would only tend to draw artillery fire, especially as the Germans still had another three weeks for aerial reconnaissance. How much use they proved to be I do not know as fortunately I was elsewhere at the time. If only the higher command had constructed some decent concrete M.G. posts at tactical points arranged in depth, like the Germans had in the north, I'm sure the retreat of March 21st would not have been anything like so costly to us. There was no excuse for we had plenty of warning. The German night bombing on our hutment camp and dumps was increasing and must have had considerable effect on the morale of the troops. I took the opportunity while here to make a few visits to the old Somme battle front around Flers, Les Boeufs and Le Transloy where we had connected with the French. It was very interesting to view the field of battle from the German positions. Although every yard of ground had been hard fought for and well churned up grass was already growing thickly over all and it was difficult to trace any particular trench line. A few peasants were about inspecting the remains of their properties with a view to a fresh start, but their hopes were soon to be dashed once more.

❖

March 1st

I received orders to proceed to the 3rd Army School of Signalling at Pas en Artois for a six-week course. This was great news.

❖

March 2nd

On 2/3/18 I proceeded with my servant by train from Achiet le Grand to Mondicourt; reporting at the school H.Q. which was in the chateau at Pas late that night. As I was one of the first to arrive for this course I was detailed to make arrangements for the messing in an empty house allotted us in the village. All officers were billeted, my own billet being an estaminet on the Mondicourt Road.

It was nice to be among the civilian population again and feel that one was so far away from trouble with not even an aeroplane to worry us at night. The school work was conducted in the chateau grounds, and huts had been built for class rooms for lectures. German prisoners of war were doing the odd jobs about the place.

❖

March 21st

On 21/3/18 the storm broke. We could hear the distant rolling thunder of the guns but could get no definite news as to how the battle was going and the school went on as usual until Saturday afternoon 23/3/18. I well remember that on that afternoon I went for a lovely walk in the direction of Hebuterne; the weather and the country were grand. Why I took that direction I do not know. Perhaps it was the sound of the guns and the desire for information, but everyone I met stopped and chatted; the one desire of all was to get to know something and no reliable information could be obtained from anyone. As yet there was no movement in this district of the civil population towards the rear, neither did we see any troops moving forward to support. When I arrived back at Pas, without any telling, I knew we were for it. The village was full of officers and all the civil population were on their door steps. The order was "pack up and stand by". Later that evening orders were posted to the effect that the school was to be disbanded and we were all to return to our units next day, Sunday 24/3/18. As so many C.Os were asking for their Signals Officer back, this was a bit of a tale. There was also a paragraph on the general situation. Quite reassuring of course, but reading between the lines one realised that the Boche was through. Only the Third Army (of which we were a part) was making anything like a shew of resistance to the north of the gap. We had our last good meal and retired to pack. The mess president had some job to settle his accounts. He had a pile of stuff on hand to last to the end of the course and the army canteen would not take it back so he had to job it off cheap among the civvies. In consequence our mess bills were very hot and most of us left in the morning with very little spare cash; at such a time, this was to be another trial to many who like myself were destined to wander about for many a day in search of our scattered units.

❖

March 24th

We all left Pas about 9.30am and marched to Doullens station where we boarded a train and proceeded via Amiens and Buire to Albert. At Buire siding we were held up for some considerable time and soon had an indication of the rot that had set in. Thousands of Labour Corps troops were straggling past; mostly Chinks and Dagos who had been employed cleaning up the old Somme battlefields. We reached Albert about 5pm and enquired of the R.T.O. our destination. He was very worried, the train was booked to Aichet le Grand but this place was now reported in German hands so we just messed about the station while the R.T.O. tried to get some definite orders from the authorities back at Amiens.

At dusk dozens of German planes came over to bomb our lines of communication and complete our discomfort. Albert came in for a good share of this heavenly stuff and we got very jumpy; more than a thousand men with two or three trains were held up near the station a fine target for Jerry. We held a pow-wow with the R.T.O. and decided the best thing to do was to get out and take up a position in defence of the town while we awaited orders. Many of us knew the ground well, having been here in 1916, so it was all arranged and just as we were moving off someone made the awful discovery that we hadn't a round of ammunition between us (it being the custom to hand it in to stores before proceeding on a course). A hasty search was made for S.A.A. among the stores at the station but none could be found. Had we found some, Albert might have been saved and the course of the war altered, for we were fit and full of fight. But without ammunition we might as well go home. We then got the men away from the station on to the high ground to the north and lay down in artillery formation as being the best protection against attack from the air. Meanwhile, the R.T.O. tried to get into communication with the authorities way back and eventually at about 10pm orders came for all details and any stragglers to proceed to Corbie for the night.

We moved off at intervals, each officer taking about 40 other ranks under his command, through Albert, a town falling to pieces and lit up only by the bursting of bombs. It was like the last days of Pompeii so I should imagine. I thought that I knew the way, but it was most difficult picking one's way between heaps of fallen masonry with telegraph lines down across the roads tripping one up, or cutting one across the face.

Transport lay in heaps obstructing the endless stream of sweating, cursing troops all making for the Amiens Road, the main line of retreat. Mixed up with this mass of disorganised troops of all units, were the remnants of the French civilian population who were at last forced to leave their houses after sticking it through nearly four years of war so near the front line. These civilians were all pushing perambulators on which they had stacked their most important possessions, these possessions invariably included a feather bed, the French peasants' most cherished possession. Most of these people had children with them, those of any age were helping their parents with the pushing or pulling of the perambulators, the others were usually perched on the feather bed. Not a murmur came from these people as they trudged on hour after hour along the side of the paved road. A few of these poor people were given a lift in G.S. wagons but however sorry we may have been for them we couldn't help much. It was war; and our first duty was to get the troops back in as good order as possible.

In passing I should mention the work of the traffic control posts, a job usually a sinecure given to men disabled or wanting a rest. Tonight 25/3/18 they were doing a great work, particularly in Albert. We arrived at Corbie in the early hours of the morning. The men were put under lock and key with a sentry. Officers were treated better; I found a billet and had a sleep and a shave and scrounged some breakfast. My fool of a servant got himself locked in the pen with other stragglers and I had great difficulty in getting him out; he proved himself a blithering old idiot and from now on until I finally lost him, he was no use or ornament. If only I had had an old soldier for a servant my lot would have been much easier. Thousands of stragglers had arrived in Corbie during the night – the square was full of them – those who were not sleeping were trying to scrounge some food. A few staff officers were trying to sort them out, but as they still came rolling in and were in no condition to fight they gave up the task and pushed us on again further to the rear.

❖

March 26th

I was given a large party of men belonging to the 5th Corps and ordered to take them via Franoillers and Contay to Toutencourt where I arrived about 5pm. I reported at corps H.Q. where the men were given a good meal and quarters for the night.

I went into No. 3 mess and met an old friend 2nd-Lt Cleave who had been a L/Cpl in 2/6 R Wks R with my platoon. He was now in a Cyclists Company attached to corps H.Q. The staff captain of 5th Corps told me that they had lent the 19th Division to the corps on their left and that they (corps) were not in touch with their other divisions but hoped for definite news of them in the morning as the cyclists were now out trying to get in touch. That was a fine state of affairs; corps not in touch with its divisions, someone must have been moving pretty quick.

❖

March 27th

In the afternoon I was sent via Acheaux to the vicinity of Louvencourt arriving about dusk; there was no one to report to and no one cared so I fixed my men up in close billets for the night and scrounged them some food. The other officer and myself had a doss down in a hovel inhabited by two of the lousiest peasants I've ever met. They were kind however and got us some bacon and egg for breakfast next morning, for which we gave them 5fr. They must have thought it a fortune judging by the profuse thanks we received.

❖

March 28th

This morning I pushed on to IV Corps at Marieux. Here an effort was again made to sort us out and do something. Fortunately for us, just as we were parading in parties, presumably to be thrown into the fight, orders were received to send all stragglers further back to Hem about 1 km west of Doullens. We pushed off, very pleased to be going in this direction, passed through Doullens and arrived at Hem about 7.30pm. On the way we passed many battalions of an Australian Division going forward. They cheered us and we them. They were quite sure that they would be able to deal with the situation. I had expected to be met at Hem by someone in authority collecting stragglers but no one was there so I had to leave my men, tired as I was, and go trudging around looking for someone to report to. I came across an H.Q. of an infantry battalion trekking forward and billeted for the night. I reported to the C.O. and explained. He of course knew nothing but was good enough to arrange for a feed for my men; no easy job at a moment's notice. I billeted my men and myself for the night in the village of Hem.

❖

March 29th

Reported again for orders in the morning and was ordered to parade my party and march to Doullens station, where we were to await a train for Frevent.

We arrived at Frevent about 5pm and here we were expected and definite arrangements made for stragglers. All my men were put with thousands of others in the grounds of a chateau with a guard on the gate, once more prisoners. Officers were allowed to go into the town and billet themselves and had to report each morning.

❖

April 1st

At 10am today a large party of us proceeded to the base by train, where we arrived about 5pm next day, 2/4/18, travelling by way of Doullens, Canaples, Vignacourt, Picquingy and Abbeville. At the latter place we stayed on the siding all night. In the morning there was time for a few officers to have a look round the city and get some breakfast. There was also time for one of my clowns to get run over by a train. Trying to get under a luggage train with a mess tin of water which he had obtained from an engine to make tea, he misjudged the speed and got a leg caught by a wheel. How he squealed; one other way of getting home to Blighty though. We were very well received at base camp; everyone was interested in us as we were the first troops through who could give the base-wallahs (as they were called) an eye witness account of the March retreat.

We had a whole day's rest to feed and re-fit. The men were able to draw some pay and I was able to cash a cheque thanks to a trusting brother officer. I was down to my last bob and couldn't get anything off the field cashier as my pay slips were in my kit – my kit I never expected to see again – and I was calculating my losses at about £30 and wishing I had gone back to the train for it at Corbie, instead of doing the right thing and helping to sort out the stragglers. However it turned up home some months later after I had invested in a new outfit.

❖

April 3rd

Orders were posted for me to leave in the morning in charge of all 19th Division stragglers and also a new draft of youngsters from home. Poor devils! What an introduction they were to have to their new unit.

❖

April 4th

Leaving the base camp about 5pm with other officers of the 19th Division, each with a draft of new and mostly young recruits, we travelled slowly as usual via Montreuil, St Pol and Hazebrouck and detrained about 1am on 5/4/18 at Caestre.

❖

April 5th

We were bundled out of the train and shepherded to an enclosure like a lot of sheep, where we slept: at least, those of us who could find some shelter slept until daylight when we got up and scrounged some sort of breakfast from men's rations given us by the remnants of an Australian division left in the camp, the division having gone south to try and stop the rot in front of Amiens. It had been a most uncomfortable night: no blankets, no fires or lights and everyone in bad humour and to make matters worse for me I discovered I had lost my servant – he must have been asleep and gone on in the train to the terminus further north. I was very fed up as I could see a lot of trouble ahead and to have to look after one's servant instead of him looking after you only adds to one's discomfort. Later in the day he arrived very bad on his feet just as I was gathering together the men of the 19th Division to proceed to our units somewhere on the Messines Ridge. Busses arrived and we proceeded. There seemed to be a gloom pass over the whole route: many of the inhabitants of these prosperous little places were gathered talking earnestly, others were packing up and leaving. In fact, most of them had already gone, estaminet keepers still hanging on to the end to do business as long as possible.

When we turned off the road to Baileul and went by way of Mt Noir which was a long way round I tackled the driver thinking he was up the pole, but he argued that it was not safe for lorries to go through Baileul. I thought he must be windy, though couldn't understand why, as there had been no action up north lately and all sounded peaceful. I had another go at him and he said Baileul had been heavily shelled lately, that the church, officers' club and the whole square were in ruins, and the inhabitants had gone. This of course accounted for the long faces of the civilians we had passed. Things were looking ominous. Over Mt Noir through Westoutre to Hyde Park Corner near Locre we went and no further would this driver go. I argued and I threatened but he said "orders is orders". As all the other drivers were of the same mind we had to foot it the rest of the way and we did just not realise how far it was from Locre to Neuve Eglise, our destination.

The men were very much out of condition and quite a number of them had been in retreat since the 21/3/18 with only a couple of days rest – if train journeys in France could be called rest. They needed very tactful handling to get them to Neuve Eglise in anything like one party and it must have taken us between three and four hours to cover the 7km to Neuve Eglise. No shelling on the way and no new shell holes and I cursed those lorry drivers again and again.

───────── ❖ ─────────

April 6th

Arriving at Neuve Eglise about 1am, an MP on duty directed us to our respective quartermasters and I personally had a very uncomfortable sleep without kit in an empty house, till late in the morning, when I saw Rossiter, our Q.M. who told me the battalion had gone straight into the line in front of Messines the day they had arrived. The Q.M. told me to report to battalion H.Q. the following morning, so I spent the rest of the day having a look at the country in the direction of Nieppe as I thought it might be useful. Here the country shewed no new shell holes and the reserve line of trenches appeared to be in quite good order and well wired, there was no firing to speak of by either side and my spirits began to rise again. The only thing that struck me was the scarcity of troops; but I knew we held the ridge and the high ground of Hill 63 behind our old front line of 1916. It never entered my head that there would be little chance of defending these lines as when the attack came the Boche rolled up our lines from the south. While on the Leinster Road (toward Romerin) I saw one of our heavies beautifully camouflaged in a farm building; on examination the whole building proved to be of collapsible stage scenery and the gun appeared only when firing.

───────── ❖ ─────────

April 7th

In the morning I took a party of some 300 men as replacements up to battalion H.Q. then at Lumm Farm (0 26d 1.7) about 1500x N of Messines, another new draft of youngsters having arrived in the morning. Poor devils, most of them only lasted three days. We went up in fighting order (suspicious this) with the ration party as guides, also carrying the first post received by the battalion since 21/3/18. Going through Wulverghem and Messines to Lumm Farm which proved to be a really good German pill box with room for all H.Q. Company and very comfortable. It was fitted up with tables and wire mattress sleeping accommodation; the signal dugout in which I was interested had buried cables to all parts and also a power buzzer and amplifier. The battalion front extended from the Wambeek in the north to the Blausepoortbeek in the south. This ground was only about 1000x south of the line taken by us on 7/6/17.

Col. Heath was still in command with Maj. Brindley (adj.). Also at battalion H.Q. was Maj. A.S. Fitzgerald (2nd in C) Lt Oakley(ass. adj.) Lt Durety (Scouts) and myself (Signals). We spent a peaceful night with the usual tours of duty.

❖

April 8th

In the morning I made a tour of company H.Qs to see my signallers and company commanders and incidentally to have a drink with same. Visual signalling communication (by lamp) was fixed up with advanced brigade H.Q. in Messines in case of eventualities; and in the afternoon Lt Durety and myself had a good look at Boche land from Signal post at approx 0 26d 9.9. The country looked beautiful and very peaceful; birds singing and not a shot fired, quieter than we had ever known a front line before, no sign of movement could be seen behind the German lines even with glasses, not the slightest indication of the storm that was brewing. At mess in the evening Col. Heath was in the best of humour considering all his troubles of the last few weeks and when whisky was passed round Maj. Brindley absentmindedly poured his into a mug and Heath thinking he had rather over-done it, poured it into a glass which it nearly filled. We had a good laugh at Brindley who is such an abstemious soul.

❖

April 9th

In the morning there was an ominous rumble over away towards Armentiers and we watched with fearful interest the sausage balloons of the enemy getting further and further through on our right. The brigade post arrived and Brindley and Fitzgerald started chewing things over quietly with the C.O. and we juniors faded away as we could see we were not wanted and the C.O. looked irritable and wanted space as usual. When we thought it safe to poke our noses into H.Q. dugout again we found the C.O. had gone to brigade and the adjutant writing out orders to the O.C. Companies; still not a word to us juniors and we felt we should have had a situation explained to us. We didn't at all like this air of mystery. The night arrived and tours of duty were arranged and I well remember getting chewed up for being a pessimist because I said we should all soon be on duty.

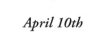

April 10th

About 3am the Boche started a general strafe, but as we had good cover it didn't worry us much but the poor companies in the open were getting it badly in the neck. The lines consisting chiefly of posts in short stretches of shallow trench: very damp and no dugouts. The covering field artillery were getting it hot too, with plenty of gas shells judging by the sound. Had we known for certain that they were gas shells we should have also have known that an attack was imminent, as it was the general practice of the Boche at that time to shell the ground behind the infantry with gas and H.E. before he launched his infantry attack.

The morning dawned fine and very misty, gradually clearing later. The shelling continued but not one casualty at H.Q. so far. All the telephones line held excepting the one to brigade. Fitzgerald now in command, spoke to each company and I believe that our front line was still intact. About 8am Capt. Brook arrived with a runner. Both looked scared and very much out of breath, and told us that the Staffords on our right had given way and that the Boche had got his company H.Q. at 0 27c 1.9 and were apparently trying to widen the gap by pressing our companies up northward. He had left Capt. Martineau with the doctor and other stretcher cases and they had all been captured. (Capt. Martineau died as a prisoner-of-war a few days later.)

Capt. Brook advised the C.O. to move and it was some time before Lt Durety and myself discovered that we were left behind; as the C.O. left to find a new H.Q. with the adjutant and the assistant adjutant without saying a word to us. Rather a shabby trick we thought, so we talked things over and I decided to stick it out (being senior) and I remember ordering the ends of the trench to be blocked up, and extra ammunition and rations issued from the reserve store which would be exposed to the enemy later on. We made a fairly defensive position and all stood to with fixed bayonets and prepared for the end, and I have no doubt that had we been left alone we could have held up the Boche till dark, as by now the shelling had passed over and their barrage was falling about 200x in our rear.

We had spotted a few Boche getting up out of the mist and firing Very Lights, apparently to mark their most forward line which was then approximately the duck board track about 0 26d 2.2 to 0 26d 6.6, when, just as the fun was starting, the C.O. sent a runner to tell us to retire to the new H.Q. at Pick House, 0 26a 4.5 – and incidentally to bring his trench coat which in his haste he had left behind. Much to our disgust we had to obey orders and while Durety and I hurriedly destroyed some H.Q. papers, and packed others into a sandbag to take away; one of the H.Q. sergeants came to me with a Boche prisoner, a very poor specimen with teeth chattering and all of a doo-da. He was in a most complete state of funk, but his pockets were full of egg bombs. It appeared that he had ventured a little ahead of his pals and one of our sergeants seeing him, dashed out and put the breeze up him. We sent him with a runner back to the rear as I thought that information might be had from him as to the German objective. This runner also took back the sandbag of orderly room papers of which there was quite a lot, as Brindley thinking we were here for a quiet time had brought up a lot of work which had got into arrears during the March retreat. The runner and his prisoner were lucky enough to meet Col. Heath in a car in Wulverghem and so our solitary prisoner was rushed off to brigade in state. Now a very different and dangerous half hour was in front of us for we had to retire when in close contact with the enemy and I for one was very windy; but we had to get going and the quicker the better.

I started them off three or four at a time to follow the C.O.'s servant; the first 50x or so was safe as H.Q. covered them from view; and we fired at imaginary Boche just to get their attention. Lt Durety and myself followed in rear and by the time we got in view of the Boche we had to walk through a storm of rifle bullets from Boche who were less than 200x away; fortunately for us, they were all a rotten lot of shots and none of us got hit. We kept to the duck board track as although more exposed we could get along much quicker than in the shell-pocked ground at the side; we refused to run, but didn't half step it. The C.O.'s party had not been so fortunate as we passed one of his runners dead by the side of the track. Later we discovered that Sig.

Higgs and Lt Oakley's servant were missing; they had been told to destroy the telephone instruments before leaving and must have got killed or taken prisoner. Once over the crest we breathed again though not for long. We met Capt. Brook with a few men taking up a line about 100x west of the Wytschaete–Messines Road by an eighteen-pounder battery, which appeared to be the only one left in action. We could see in the valley to the west dozens of batteries, including heavies with tractors, withdrawing out of action. This withdrawal had apparently been going on all night and accounted for the fact that we had no support from our guns. The infantry and forward batteries were to be sacrificed as usual; Poor Bloody Infantry let down again. And all the ground we had sacrificed so much to gain in 1917 had to be given up without a fight. We couldn't understand this at the time as we didn't know then to what depth the enemy had penetrated on the Hazebrouck front. The gunners of this exposed battery asked us where the front line was and what to fire at and I'm sure had rather a shock when we told them that we were all that remained of their front-line infantry. They decided to stick it and later in the day were firing over open sites as the Boche tried to come over the ridge.

We found the C.O. and adjutant in a shanty by the side of the road at Pick House 0 26a 5.6 and here we sorted out H.Q. Company and took up a line in an old German communication trench running east from the road. There was a good field of fire but little cover. Then down came the Boche barrage of heavy stuff again and we found we were just in it properly. Ten minutes of this and none of us would have been left so I suggested to the C.O. that it would be better to either go forward or back a little. I preferred going forward as by going back we should soon have been in the Boche line of fire when he increased his range as he surely would later. However, the C.O. preferred to go back. We got back at a good pace as there were no Boche to see us hurry and though we had some very near shaves from heavy shells which nearly knocked us down they burst so close, we managed to get back to a decent cellar in north H.Q. 0 19b 9.9 leaving a sentry on guard on top we stayed here till evening. While here, Lt Durety again got in touch with Capt. Brook and his party and I got in touch with the battalion on our left whose H.Q.s were in a wood; they were the 1st Wiltshires and their front line had not been attacked as yet but there was a huge gap on their right flank. They didn't seem to worry as they were being relieved that night, so they thought, but I'm sure they were disappointed as their relief must have by now been used up elsewhere.

Toward evening Australian scouts began to arrive, stealthily creeping forward to find the gaps in our line; they also counter-attacked Messines village and took it but were soon driven out again. During the night we moved back to some hutments just off the Vierstraat Road in Grand Bois, about 0 13c 4.9, as the C.O. evidently wished to keep his H.Q. intact and not get them captured if the Boche pressed his attack again in the morning. We slept a little and had some food which we begged, washed and shaved and felt much better and Durety and I were sent to find a suitable position for H.Q. about N 23d 9.5, which place would be nearer to Capt. Brook's party and incidentally on our correct front.

❖

April 11th

It was a lovely morning and we had a nice walk: just enough shelling to make things interesting. We found a suitable place for H.Q. in our old front line of 1917; we reported back to H.Q. and brought them here for the rest of the day. Rations arrived for which we were very thankful and my fool servant also, he having got lost the previous day and had gone back to transport lines to find himself. We also learnt that the battalion had been reinforced by all the spare men from transport lines under a Col. McCordich who was with us for a few days for instruction – a Cook's tour, hope he enjoyed it. We did not rest here long but moved again in the night to old front line of 1917 by Spanbroekmolen where I was given command of a composite company and H.Q. quartered for the night in a farmhouse at about N 29c 2.9 (D'Hoing Farm). There were minor attacks in the morning of 12/4/18 but could not see anything from my position in reserve by the mine crater of Spanbroekmolen. There was little shelling as the Boche was probably moving his guns forward and the front line held. Later in the day I was ordered to take my company back to reserve line of trenches and here spent rest of the day and next evening.

❖

April 13th

We were heavily shelled by 5.9 all the morning but had no serious casualties, which was extraordinary considering the amount of heavy stuff that came our way. Troops began to come up and go past us forward: new recruits mostly and none seemed clear as to where they were to go. We could see the Germans coming over the ridge by Neuve Eglise, or they may have been British troops in retreat, we never really knew. We could see German batteries firing at us and we just waited and hoped to be relieved before the next real assault came. I well remember in 1917 viewing these reserve lines of ours at the foot of Kemmel Hill and thinking how lovely it would be to defend them, but now the time had arrived they didn't seem so inviting. During the day, orders came to take up a line in an old communication trench (Regent Street) facing south with our right on the Kemmel to Neuve Eglise Road by Lindenhock Corner. This was a complete change of front and we realised that the line was being reorganised and that the Boche were probably in Neuve Eglise. We were instructed that this line was to be the front line and all troops in front were passing through until midnight, after that we were to expect the Boche and were responsible for the defences of this line. My servant never arrived here and though we searched for him, he was lost for good this time – must have got pinched by the Boche as he was so slow on his feet. We found quite a good dug out for company H.Q. and although we had been on the alert we managed to get a real sleep in turn. Although we had not seen a German near we knew he had followed close on our heels and by morning his machine guns were located quite near; he was very clever at quietly following up without being seen, particularly his machine gunners.

❖

April 14th

This morning there was a terrific action taking place in and around Neuve Eglise and our fellows were finally driven out. We watched the Boche fire creeping forward and our men retiring back over the ridge and German guns coming in to action in the valley about Squares T 11 and 12. We had a look around this morning to gain touch with our other companies and to get a general idea of the situation. We explored some old houses as we thought they might be suitable for H.Q. but when 5.9s started dropping around we decided it was a very unhealthy spot and beat it back to Lindenhock Corner. Later in the morning a message arrived bringing tidings of our promised relief and also that some of our brigade had counter-attacked that morning and taken eleven prisoners. This was just to keep our spirits up of course as what was eleven against the thousands we had lost? But we made the most of it when we retold it to the men. The French arrived with much chatter about

10am. I believe we were the first to be relieved. They were big fellows from the south of France and by their chatter we gathered that we were a poor lot to lose so much ground; but later, when the Boche started his evening strafe and dropped his stuff all along the road behind the trench it was likened to Verdun. I borrowed 2nd-Lt Beaufoy from one of our companies to help in the takeover as I couldn't speak a word of French as they spoke. Their officers were very efficient fellows and wanted to know everything: much more than we could tell them, particularly they wanted to know where our machine guns were. But of these we could tell them nothing; they were rightly disgusted. Divisional machine gun companies were acting independently – if acting at all? We never thought much of them.

Among other things handed over were about six gallons of rum sent up to put fight into the troops. It was very amusing to see the Frogies try to drink rum; they batted their eyes and choked and soon decided it was "no bon", so we poured it away as being too much trouble to carry out and too risky to leave behind in case some got hold of it and took too much and became "beaucoup zigzag". We explained by actions.

The French were to be responsible for the defence after 12 noon but we were not able to leave until later and it was late in the evening before we said 'au revoir' to the frogs and dragged our weary way back through the village of Kemmel, across the open to Hyde Park Corner and thence to Westoutre and finally dossing down for the night in an old barn about G 25b 4.2 just west of the road to Poperinghe. It was nerve-racking night for the first few hundred yards as the road to Kemmel was being swept by machine gun fire in enfilade and the men were so dog tired it was difficult to get a move on; some were so bad that when we got to a piece of sunken road at approximately N 20d 6.3 they refused to go further without a rest. It was a most unhealthy spot; a sunken road, lately churned up by shell fire, enfiladed from Messines Ridge. Anywhere but here, I told them. I tried coaxing and I tried cursing and my own mouth was becoming dry from fright as I expected the Boche to start shelling any minute. They fell asleep and we others were forced to leave them, as we dare not run the risk of staying here with my company. They never arrived in camp and to save awkward explanations they were just returned as missing. On we went to Hyde Park Corner, all straggling along, when we were stopped by some staff officers who asked who we were. We replied by asking who the devil they were anyway and saying "its no business of yours". I fingered my revolver and we all looked pretty desperate, especially as we had five days growth of beard. They were sensible fellows and realised immediately that we doubted their identity and that we were not in the right humour to be fooled. By the aid of a torch we recognised our brigade major and explanations quickly followed. He was there for the purpose of stopping any men retiring, except the 10th R Wks R, who were of course relieved. The morale was so bad that men were conveniently getting lost and retiring on their transport lines, he told us. We of course had thought for a moment that he was a German spy trying to cause trouble and getting to know our units, as they were reported to have done on the Somme, it being so unusual to meet staff officers prowling round such places in the dead of night.

❖

April 16th

We only stayed here until the morning of 16/4/18 and then marched back to an old hutment camp near Proven, 16km from Ypres. It was the dirtiest camp we had ever been in, but we were able to get a clean up and a rest. We were not very particular so long as we were away from the shelling. This camp wasn't shelled while we were there though a few express ones came to rest just east of the main road: just near enough to keep us interested. While here I was fortunate enough to get a day off to go by lorry to St Omer, where I was able to get some new kit from Ordance as mine had gone west when I left it behind in the train at Albert on 24/5 March and for the last three weeks had had to manage with what I carried on my back which increased the misery of my existence considerably.

St Omer was almost deserted of civilians, such a contrast to the busy place we had known it as previously. On the way back our bus was nearly hit by a shell as we came near the railway sidings just south of "Pop ". This promiscuous shelling was always going on now and one was never really safe, though these stray ones did little damage except to our nervous system. While here it appeared in orders that I had taken over pay and command of "D" Company, now only about 70-strong. The battalion was reorganised as well as possible, each company being about the same strength. The battalion must have lost over 400 since the morning of 10/4/18.

❖

April 25th

About 3am I experienced once again that awful sinking feeling which I suppose only comes to the windy. I was awakened at this hour when one's vitality is so low, by an orderly vigorously shaking me in my valise and asking me if I was O.C. "D" Company. He produced a message from H.Q. the content of which I knew without looking. It was as usual – 'the C.O. will see all officers immediately'. By the aid of a torch I pulled on some trousers and boots and over all, my trench coat and went with the other officers to H.Q. There was little news, except that the Boche was expected to make another push and that we were to go forward in reserve and lorries would be waiting for us in half an hour's time. I instructed Sgt-Maj. Shoebottom to parade the company in fighting order immediately and got the servants to scramble round and produce some tea and sandwiches. To turn out on such an errand on an empty belly would have been too awful. The lorries duly arrived and we embussed and were rushed off to Lord knows where. I was not at all happy with my command; the men were half asleep and grousing very little, which was a bad sign. In fact they seemed lifeless: few knew their officers and we knew less of the men. It was fortunate that there still survived a few old sweats – the type who never die. They did their best to cheer things up.

We debussed at Ouderdom G 30a and marched to a farm at G 36a 1.7 passing on the way a few Boche prisoners, who in the dim light of dawn seemed to have a smirk on their dials; something was going on ahead, the guns were all busy and the ground between us and Ypres was thick with troops.

During the morning O.C. Companies went forward to reconnoitre the ground between La Clytte and Dickebusch, as we were expecting to get pushed into a counter attack at any moment as that morning the French had lost Kemmel Hill and the Boche were reported to be in Locre. We passed several batteries of French 75mm and a number of French wounded coming back. These frogs make war look picturesque and almost romantic; when a shell bursts among them you hear a lot of jabber and shouts of "Vive la France" as they pop off with renewed energy; so unlike our chaps who just curse and blast.

When we got back to our companies we were heavily shelled as was only to be expected now that the Boche had perfect observation from Kemmel Hill and because we had been stuck near a railway siding where a 12-inch naval gun of ours had been firing at intervals all morning. This gun had been a great source of interest to our boys, but we knew the Boche would make a great effort to silence it.

❖

April 26th

The Boche plastered this spot and the gun was withdrawn by an R.O.D. engine and us poor B's were left to pay. It got so hot that I asked the C.O. for permission to move my company to the other side of the railway where it was safer. Here we got into some slits in the ground and only had one casualty, whereas the others who stayed back in the farmyard suffered severely, losing about 25 killed and wounded including Lt O'Neill (killed) and Capt. Brook and another officer wounded and all to no purpose as we were only in reserve and surely it couldn't have made much difference to move 100x or so to a safer place. Our losses being so high and our morale so low that in the evening division ordered us back to camp at Proven to remain in reserve there and to be ready to move at a moment's notice. We marched back to camp via Busseboom and Poperinghe arriving in the early morning of 27/4/18.

❖

April 29th

We were not left in peace long and were moved in the early morning of 29/4/18 to lie in reserve about 2000x west of Reningkeist G 32d. Here the only thing of interest was the roast pig we had for dinner; the farmer in his haste to get away had left behind a couple of young pigs and our chaps having nothing to do and being fed up with life started chasing these pigs round for fun. But when the H.Q. mess cook appeared on the scene he suggested pork for dinner and that was the end of the pigs, but new pig is awful and we suffered. The other item was the appearance of an old French peasant with his Madame talking nineteen to the dozen and gesticulating like a semaphore. We couldn't understand a word: they only made us laugh and they got in a rage and left, reappearing later with a French interpreter who explained that in their haste to get clear with their livestock, they had left behind 200 French francs. On enquiry being made the lost money was handed over to them by Capt. Kentish, the money having being found by one of his men and handed over to him. I believe Madame in her joy kissed the captain, or tried to, and was loud in her praises of "Les Soldats Anglaise".

❖

May 1st

We were moved across country further north near Busseboom G 16b where we bivouacked or found what shelter we could. Strange to say, this district was quite restful, although there were some of our heavy 8-inch Howitzers near by, but as they had only lately arrived the Boche had not yet found them.

❖

May 3rd

On the afternoon of 3/5/18, Company Command had to make another reconnaissance of the ground just west of Dickebusch. There was supposed to be a good reserve line here lately dug out but we couldn't find it: only a few slits in the ground very disconnected. Evidently the working party had been dispersed by the Boche fire, but all the same had reported having completed their task. We didn't let them down. As soon as we arrived back at our companies we received orders to take them up to this new line. This was some journey for the officers as the three trips totalled about 10 miles for the afternoon – hard-going under these conditions.

We proceeded just before dusk via Ouderdom, on the way our S.O.S was seen to go up all along our front (red over green over yellow) and all the artillery opened up one sheet of flames and smoke. At last we were really making a shew; it was deafening but very thrilling, but I was fearful lest the Boche should drop his heavy stuff on us before we got into position. To have got my company scattered and lost the first time I took them into action would have taken some living down. I tried to hurry the men on but they were all getting jumpy and it was impossible to make oneself heard, so had to leave the men at intervals to direct. Fortunately the German fire did not come our way and we managed to get into our holes though we didn't know which way to face, the situation was so obscure. Later we heard that the Boche had again been repulsed in front of Locre; just one more effort on his part to penetrate between the Scherpenberg and Mont Rouge. We stood to for hours, expecting at any moment to be overrun, but nothing happened and when it poured with rain we got into some hutments and had a rest.

❖

May 4th

We had an early breakfast but, as soon as it was light, shells began to fall all round and we beat it pretty quick back to our holes in the ground, which, though so uncomfortable on account of the wet were far safer. We watched all day the hutments going up in the air and splinters flying all over the place, but we escaped – not a single casualty. It was a most miserable day; it rained and rained and we couldn't get rid of the water from our short trenches and we dare not get out as we were under observation. I remember reminding company Q.M.S. Haseler how we had played at digging trenches in the garden at home, when school boys together, but he didn't seem to think the comparison funny. The Boche seemed to be making a dead set at what remained of the village of Dickebusch which was now a smouldering ruin and I wondered how the other companies were faring, who were in trenches just east of it; and we also wondered how we should get to their support if wanted. I suppose I should have made a reconnaissance but felt sure no one could have crossed the Dickebusch to Locre Road and kept a whole skin. So we remained in our holes in the ground, improving them as best we could and we stayed here another night and no orders came for us to counter-attack.

❖

May 5th

Rations came up and orders also arrived for us to take up a new line further back at H 19d 9.5 near where Maj. Brindley (now in command) at his battalion H.Q. Of course we were all pleased it was back and not forward, but in the pitch darkness of the night it was most difficult to trail across country without a guide or previous reconnaissance and it seemed to take hours to do little over 2000x. We kept falling over barbed wire and getting mixed up with other troops going in or out and had many nasty shocks from our batteries which we couldn't see until under the very noses of the guns. We arrived, very worked up, reported to HQ and spent a comfortable quiet day (6/5/18) in these new trenches.

❖

May 7th

Next day was the same until evening when we had to report to R.Es for digging a new line of trench, which was behind a battery of French guns. I was glad to have something definite to do as sitting and thinking and wondering when you might have to do a counter-attack makes one get more windy every minute. When finished I turned in to have a sleep in a barn nearby where my company was entrenched. I had what remained of my company H.Q. with me and there were other odds and ends from other units taking their chance of a comfortable sleep. This barn was part of the farm building where battalion H.Q. was.

May 8th

About 3am on 8/5/18 the Germans opened up with heavy stuff on the French battery behind us, which up to now had not been shelled at all and neither had this farm building. This outburst of shell fire woke us up and while collecting our thoughts and trying to make up our minds whether to risk it and go to sleep again or get into the trenches outside, a heavy shell came through the roof of the building and burst on the chaff covered floor among the sleeping men. The confusion was terrible – most of us half asleep, and in pitch darkness the place was filled with fumes and thick with dust raised by the explosion. There was a scramble for the door and some shouted that it was gas. There were cries and groans from the wounded and I gave orders for my men to collect their things and get into the trenches with the rest of the company. A piece of shell had hit me in the hand and didn't half sting and when we managed to get a light and started to collect our things I felt something warm running down my pants and sleeve and on investigation discovered it was blood. Couldn't make it out at first as the wound in the hand was only slight; I had however been pretty badly hit in other places but in the excitement I had not noticed it. Oh! Joy – a Blighty one and so convenient too!

To get one a couple of miles from the line was just what we all prayed for; easy to get away with. As soon as my men had got clear of the barn I trotted off to the aid post with 2nd-Lt Richards who had also stopped a piece. Richards' luck was out, for just as we were tumbling into the aid post another shell burst behind us and poor Richards stopped another which unfortunately killed him, as two days later he died in the C.C.S. at Arneke having had a leg amputated.

The M.O. patched us up and just as I was feeling queer and going to faint the sentry on the door cried 'Gas!' and I knew that to lose consciousness now would have been to lose hope, so pulled myself together and managed to get my gas bag on, and there I lay for what seemed hours striving to keep conscious and all the time fit to burst; the heat in a gas mask is terrific. I prayed and I cursed the Boche alternately, I did so want a peaceful half hour so that we wounded could get further back. At last the shelling ceased and we waited for what seemed hours before we could get taken back to the A.D.S. While waiting I heard that the shell that fell in the barn had killed two and wounded fourteen. It left my company without an officer or senior N.C.O. as C.Q.M.S. Haseler had also been badly hit.

At last R.A.M.C. cars arrived to take away the stretcher cases; 2nd-Lt Richards and myself, one above the other in the same tin lizzy. These R.A.M.C. chaps then left us in the car while they had a cup of tea. I got fairly worked up; they didn't know what we had just been through and might have to go through again at any moment. Why didn't they get a move on, the fools, messing about like this? And when they did appear the mess cook appeared also: would I like to wait while he made me a cup of tea? To hell with the tea – kind thought though, and I tried to thank him nicely but would rather get a move on and so, after saying good-bye to a few men hovering round and looking envious, we moved off. Got an awful shaking up, and had to hold on tight to the side of the stretcher with my undamaged hand to keep from rolling off.

It was a lovely morning and I tried to raise myself up and take notice; life was beginning to be really worth living again, though my wounds were now beginning to pain, my leg having gone quite stiff. Still, I didn't care, felt perfectly safe now and I began to have visions of home and sick leave and the promenade at Bournemouth. Our first stop was at the Advance Dressing Station near Busseboom. While waiting to be dealt with, Sgt-Maj. Brown (old Solihull boy) of the Div. R.A.M.C. appeared to take particulars of the cases and relieve us of ammunition, bombs etc. I asked him if he could leave me alone as I was comfortable and didn't want to be messed up by another M.O. but had to go through in my turn; but they only took off the field dressings and squirted some antiseptic into the wounds. When we were all waiting for our next move back, dear old Fr Rocliffe S.J. appeared on the scene and promised to write home for us. Lt Richards by this time was very bad and delirious and his carrying on made us feel very sad, otherwise everything in the garden was lovely. Our next stop was at a dressing station near Proven; here they only dealt with those who were obviously very bad, we others got a good feed and waited till evening and then were sent to the Casualty Clearing Station at railhead near Arneke. Crowds of wounded were here, rows and rows of stretchers lay in tents waiting their turn for the operating theatre. Orderlies came round taking particulars of the red ticket cases of which I was one and we were prepared for the theatre. The others no doubt had a good feed and a sleep as they could not possibly have been attended that night there were so many. At last my turn came and on the slab I went.

———— ❖ ————

May 9th

Woke up late next day having had a lovely sleep and lovely dreams; found myself in a large marquee with beds down each side and a basin to be sick in at the side of the bed, which in my case was not wanted as I felt fine. But why was I stuck to the bed; surely I hadn't done anything? Then a nurse appeared, the first fair lady I had seen for over five months and I was all confused. She asked how I felt, was I feeling sick or hungry? She brought some tea and sandwiches and then started to change the undersheet, I had a squint at it and found it was only blood, what a relief. Next night was disturbed by German planes dropping bombs but they were not very near; probably they were after the railway sidings, not the hospital. Poor Richards opposite, kept waking us up with his groans, he was very near the end.

———— ❖ ————

May 10th

In the morning we who were fit were evacuated to the base hospitals, I went to No. 14 General at Wimereaux; here I was operated on again and my wounds sewn up (they had been left open at the C.C.S.). D.P.S. it was called and my ticket had been marked accordingly. After a few more inoculations for typhus, tetanus etc. I was finally put aboard a boat for dear old Blighty.

———— ❖ ————

May 13th

I arrived in England 13/5/18 where I was sent to 1/5 Northern General Hospital at Leicester. On being unloaded from the train at Leicester we passed through a crowd of nosey parkers: even after four years of war a hospital train was still a first class entertainment for the masses. The hospital was a converted lunatic asylum, a very appropriate place for subalterns of infantry, next war it's the A.S.C. for me. Stayed here about six weeks and had the time of my life. We were treated as officers and not like schoolchildren as we had been at Worsley Hall.

❖

June 1918

At the end of six weeks I was sent to Eaton Hall which was a decided change for the worse: rigorous discipline again and only allowed out for a couple of hours a day. We were kept in order by the threat of losing our three weeks leave on discharge.

❖

July 13th

During my three weeks leave I got married and spent my honeymoon at Stratford-upon-Avon and Llandudno and then had to report at 3rd Reserve Battalion, then stationed in barracks at Dover. I reported to the adjutant and was told to attend a lecture for all officers in the evening, but on going to my room fell fast asleep and didn't wake till after mess. Some start this! I expected an awful ticking off but fortunately had not been missed.

❖

August 1918

A few days later I arranged to live out and Doris came to Dover in August week and we fixed up in a boarding establishment. I soon had another move which was to the signal school in one of the forts, which was just to my liking: no senior officers prowling round and those of us who had seen service as signals officers overseas, were well respected and had a fine time in consequence.

While in Dover which was a closed city (passports being necessary to enter or leave) many extraordinary rules were in force, such as the wearing of our tin hats and gas masks, which was very irksome to those from the home front, but I suppose it amused General Hickie who was in command. There were also alarms when we had to man the coast defences: much cursing and swearing and no good was done as they always seemed to be a mess up, but I suppose the staff enjoyed them. While at Dover the monitor Glatton blew up and was sunk by torpedo to save the fire exploding the magazines and destroying Dover. Over 70 men were killed.

❖

October 1918

About the middle of October I was sent to Dunstable on a three month signals course, which was the premier course for the British Army; I had asked for this move as it made me sure of at least another three months at home.

While here the Armistice was signed (November 11th) amidst much rejoicing. In Dunstable the C.O. was an old dug-out who never even gave us a half day to celebrate the occasion. The colonial troops on the course took French leave, but we Britishers only grumbled. Discipline was to strong with us, but we wished afterwards that we had had more pluck, as every other military centre at home let things go and I really believe the higher command could not have blamed us.

❖

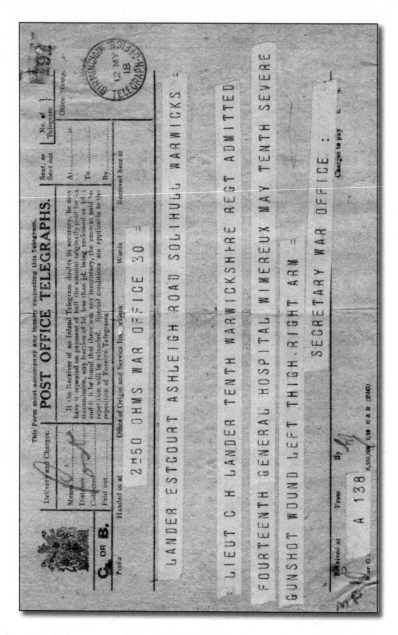

May 1918. Telegram notifying of Charles Lander's wounding and one which would see him out of harm's way for the duration. Author's collection.

Charles and Dorothy in 1918. Author's collection.

1919 and After

Portrait of Charles Lander, 1982.
Author's collection.

January 1919

The course over, I reported again to 3rd Reserve Battalion then in billets at Tunbridge Wells, nothing doing – all the life and interest had gone out of the army. Then a move for a few days to a hutment camp at Crowborough and finally we were sent to Catterick camp where I spent the last few weeks of my army life in a barn of a camp, miles from anywhere and all we were doing was just waiting for our discharge.

❖

March 17th

I left Catterick camp early on the morning of 17/3/19 with a party for demobilisation. We had to proceed to Fovant for this great event, and arrived there the same day.

❖

March 19th

I had to wait until 19/3/19 for my ticket. No demobilisation took place from units, all and everyone having to report at a demobilisation centre.

❖

1922

A few years after, an effort was made to get the boys together again. A reunion was arranged and Bingley Hall, Birmingham, taken for the evening. The shew was well advertised, but the results were very disappointing; very few turned up at the different rallying points in the hall. I'm sorry to say it developed into a booze-up. In fact, many arrived too well oiled and most of the officers left in disgust very early.

❖

1931

Early in 1931 Maj. Brindley had a brainwave and successfully arranged a smoking concert at the White Horse Hotel, Congreve Street Birmingham for officers and men of the 10th Battalion only. This was held on Monday

March 23rd and in contrast to the previous reunion this affair proved a great success. Those present included Maj. Brindley in the chair, Capts Latham and Kentish, and Lts F.P. Smith, Rose, Godsall, myself and one or two others. Many of the very first members of the battalion were present; some obviously very under the weather; but still carrying on as old soldiers never die. It was really a great evening and we arranged to meet again in November.

Afterword
Michael Harrison

Old Soldiers Never Die...

Following his discharge from the Army in 1919, Charles found himself to be a married man with prospects. His parents owned a comfortable house in Solihull and his father was well established in the manufacturing jewellery business. Like countless others, many of whom were not as fortunate as Charles, he had to make the transition from war to peace. Gone was living at the edge of life itself and often seeing his friends blotted out for ever. Gone also was the provision of food three times per day (the average recruit gained twenty-one pounds in weight) together with medical care and clothing. Britain in 1919 was a sink or swim society with the general level of well being far below that which we experience today.

Charles returned to work at the family firm only to be greeted by his father with an admonishment for enlisting in the King's service instead of which, in Mr Lander's opinion, Charles should have stayed behind to help run the firm which had been turned over to war work. How odd it must have seemed to join the ant-like scramble from the suburbs into Birmingham; thousands of former soldiers would have been making exactly the same daily struggle to the countless factories and offices of the great city. Many were not so lucky and found themselves down on their luck, living day to day in the hope of putting meals on the family table.

By 1921, Charles had purchased what would prove to be his only venture into property, which is the family home in St. Bernard's Road, Olton, where his daughter still resides to this day. Children followed to a grand total of six, including twins and his daughter Mary still recalls the wonderful, happy life that the family led. Christmas was always celebrated with great enthusiasm; Mary fondly recalls the special atmosphere in the house at Christmas, helped along by the gentle hiss of the gas lighting. The family had a love for dogs and kept several together with at least one pony. Summer would find them making a swimming party in Olton Mere. The mere is a reservoir for topping up the Grand Union canal which meanders nearby on its way to London. Never intended as a swimming venue, the mere is never warm but these were hardy souls.

It was during these escapades that Mary would notice the scar tissue on her Dad's thigh, each time he was asked by his inquisitive youngsters as to the origin of the scars he would always deny being wounded, it was put down to several things but never the Great War.

The great beast of uncertainty struck without warning when Charles arrived for work one day to be told that he was no longer employed by the family firm. In fact he was not employed at all as his father had sold the business without any discussion or warning. Thrown back on to his own resources, Charles converted one of the attics in the family home to a workshop and began to manufacture jewellery in his own right. Using his many contacts who trusted him without question, he built up a steady business selling his products to all parts of the UK. There were setbacks which he found most distressing. When staying in a hotel on the south coast of England, his two cases of samples were stolen from his hotel room, never to be seen again. One of the Birmingham firms that Charles did business with was the famous Smith and Pepper factory; the factory is now an excellent museum located in the heart of Birmingham's Jewellery Quarter. Charles almost certainly knew Sydney Pepper, a son of one of the partners. Sydney had served with the 8th Battalion Royal Warwickshires at the Somme, taking part in the disastrous attack at Serre Road on July 1st 1916; the battalion suffered a 90% casualty rate that day. Sidney was killed at Ypres the following year.

How difficult life must have been for men who had come safely home. Sometimes, perhaps in the small hours, the memories came flooding back. Old pals crowding into the ex-soldiers thoughts as the clock ticked away the lonely hours of darkness. In the light of day they would have to pass the homes of their missing friends and relatives or attend the same workplace that they had known together. Ex-servicemen who had lost limbs were a common sight on the streets and still were up to the 1950s. On two occasions Charles could have lost a limb through the whirling shell splinters: only his legendary luck saved him from possible dismemberment.

The years rolled past, old comrades met and parted once again, some back into grinding poverty. The "hungry thirties" arrived with the world in recession and millions thrown out of work. For instance ex-Lifeguards trooper, W.H. Smith of Chadwick End, some seven miles distant from Charles Lander's home, a skilled bricklayer, for some time, ex-Trp. Smith's only hope of work was to walk from Chadwick End to Halesowen, a distance of sixteen miles as the crow flies, there to join a queue of anxious hopefuls begging for a few days toil. Some reward for risking one's life for the country.

The world itself began the inexorable slide into war as politicians and diplomats dithered and fudged. Once more Charles found himself facing the awful prospect of foreign domination by a hostile nation; how, along with all parents in the United Kingdom must he have feared for his children's future?

War work was to dominate the family for years to come, Mary became a Land Girl and grew to love the life. Charles once again donned a uniform, and became a member of the Home Guard. Six years of war and fourteen years of rationing would pass before life would begin to return to something approaching normality.

I was never to have the privilege of meeting Charles although I feel that I must have passed him in the street as I frequently had to make use of the road past his front door, often several times a day. Having read and re-read his memoir and absorbing his daughter's memories of him I feel that in a small way I have got to know Lt Lander; a fair minded soul, calm and unflustered, a man in the true sense, who showed kindness to all with a towering love for his family. Charles enjoyed almost four decades of peace before he answered the final roll-call on 6th November 1984. His dear wife Dorothy (Doris) joined him two days later on 8th November; they had always declared that they would never be apart. Charles and Dorothy are buried in the cemetery of the Franciscan friary in Olton, almost opposite their family home.

So passed another Boy of the Old Brigade...*they only fade away...*

Michael Harrison, 2009.

Appendix I
Notes on Recent Operations

19th Division No. G. 48/27
Notes On Recent Operations

The following notes are the result of experience gained in the recent operations and embody the main features of the experiences of all officers down to commanding officers of units, R.E. Companies, Trench Mortar Batteries, and Machine Gun Companies. These notes are by no means exhaustive and only touch generally on subjects which require the close attention of all concerned as regards detail. If we have seen the last of trench warfare some of these notes will, for the time being at any rate, be in abeyance.

Dumps and Carrying Parties – The organisation of carrying parties and the situation of dumps worked well where the arrangements made previously were not disorganised by the unforeseen events which will always occur in any battle. The relay system was found to work very well as each carrying party acquired a knowledge of the route on its particular section. It has been put forward that badges are necessary for carriers, not only for the purpose of their identification when required, but also in order that stragglers from carrying parties proceeding to the rear without orders might be identified. Demands for stores, ammunition, etc., must be made in writing to prevent unauthorised persons making such demands, and guides must always be sent at the same time. At each forward dump where Stokes Mortar Ammunition is accumulated there should be a few men under a responsible N.C.O. or private detailed to clean and put cartridges into the bombs before they are sent up to the batteries. Some tools should form part of the advanced brigade ammunition dump, unless the position of the advanced R.E. dump coincides with the latter. As operations continue it will be possible no doubt to use mule transport for the carrying up of stores to a forward position beyond which carriers will be used for the last section of the relay line. Up to the present a complicated trench system and the lack of traffic routes with bridges over trenches has prevented the use of limbered wagons and mules for this work.

An important feature of the operations was the great use made of bombing squads. All officers are agreed that too many bombs were thrown to achieve the particular object in view. The result of throwing too many bombs is that throwers exhaust themselves unnecessarily soon, waste bombs, and put a great strain on the carrying parties which supply them. These faults may be attributed to the bombers themselves being too heavily laden with bombs, to indifferent discipline, and to lack of system when officers hurriedly organised bombing squads selected from troops who had become much mixed in the progress of the fight. It is suggested that bombers should be followed by a few Lewis guns to protect their flanks as they advance, and by Stokes Mortars to barrage enemy's communications, with a view to cutting off their supplies of bombs and prevent their being reinforced. Infantry should follow bombers to support them and if possible these should be detailed from the same unit (companies) which supplied the bombing squads. In defensive bombing a man with a few bombs should be placed as a sentry so as to give as much rest as possible to the bombing squad who should be near at hand in case the enemy should make a determined attack. In an attack across the open the bombers should not normally advance with the first line as their duties consist chiefly in "nettoyage"* and opening up lines of communication.

When carrying out an attack on a locality such as La Boisselle, or where the trench system is complicated, a definite body of troops should be detailed for the service of "nettoyage" who must not allow themselves to be drawn into the advance until their duties are completed. The troops mentioned above should be drawn from a different unit to that which is making the direct attack.

Vickers Machine Guns – Vickers Machine Guns should be used in preference to Lewis guns for the defence against counter-attack in localities which have been consolidated as they are more capable of sustained fire.

Lewis Guns – Lewis guns have shown themselves to be invaluable when taken forward with the leading infantry. They should also still continue to be used as heretofore to accompany patrols pushed forward in front of the leading infantry to make good vantage points from which a fresh advance can be initiated.

Stokes Guns – The Stokes Gun has been found invaluable in preparing the way for a fresh advance during a pause in the attack and for the defence of strong points. While troops are on the move their use is not so apparent as it takes some appreciable time to get them into action, obtain the range, and bring up ammunition.

Attacks across the open – have been found to succeed where bombing up trenches has been costly in lives and slow in execution. The sight of cold steel on troops badly shaken by a bombardment has been proved to be demoralising.

Signalling – The best use of visual signal was not made. It cannot be expected that cable will remain intact when laid across shell swept zones.

Wireless – A memorandum has been issued under this office No. I.66/2 of 13th instant as regards the use of wireless between battalion headquarters and brigade headquarters.

Liaison – (a) During active operations, liaison will always be maintained between the flank battalions of 19th Division and the nearest battalions of neighbouring formations.   (b) For this purpose the flank battalion will, as a matter of course, send a liaison officer with at least two runners to the H.Q. of the nearest battalion of the neighbouring brigade.   (c) The duties of this liaison officer will be to keep his own battalion H.Q. informed of the progress made and any operations contemplated by the battalion to which he is attached. He and the runners will be relieved in the ordinary course when his battalion is relieved.

Issue of Operation Orders – Complaints have been made that operation orders did not reach the officers for whom they were intended till it was too late to act on them.   It has been suggested by one brigade that operation orders should be issued twelve hours previously to all concerned. It will rarely be possible to do this during active operations owing to the change in situations and because of the fact that in many cases operation orders from higher formations reach Divisional Headquarters two hours or less before they have to be acted upon. In this case, all that can be done is to send out a preliminary order or message to warn all concerned that an operation is about to be initiated, the details following later. Attention is directed to the recent orders to the effect that operation orders are not to be communicated on the telephone within two miles of the front line.

Improvement of Communications – A careful marking of routes for carrying parties is one of the first duties of the R.E. The C.R.E. is arranging for a supply of "IN" and "OUT" boards for use in the trenches, the words "UP" and "DOWN" are not to be used as they are liable to be misunderstood. The marking out of an overland route by stakes and a continuous "handrail" of wire was, and always will be, invaluable. Filling in useless trenches at junctions where parties might take a wrong turning is often advisable.

Word of Command Not To Be Used – (a) It was evident in the recent operations that many soldiers in the division were unaware, or did not remember, that one of the enemy's favourite ruses is to call out 'retire' with the intention of causing our troops to pass this order and carry it out. All ranks must be warned that the word "retire" has ceased to exist, and is not to be uttered, much less obeyed, and anyone using the word is liable to be shot on the spot. (b) It is only under exceptional circumstances that troops should be called upon to withdraw. In such cases the order should emanate from an officer. The word "withdraw" should be used and a definite point or line onto which the withdrawal is to be conducted should be given. Further, the name of the officer giving the order should be indicated. An example of such an order is: 'Order from Captain STOUTHEART – Withdraw to line of road 200 yards away' (c) Brigade Commanders will please see that every man under their command is acquainted with these instructions.

Slight Wounds – Officers and other ranks who are wounded in the course of operations but whose wounds do not wholly incapacitate them, should continue taking an active part in the fight until ordered to the rear by a superior officer. In this connection it is pointed out that the presence of a wounded officer, N.C.O., or man who, though wounded, has the grit to continue fighting is a fine example of courage and most inspiring to the others.

Discarding Equipment, Rifles etc. – It has been noticed that men are in the habit of discarding their rifles and equipment when wounded. No man is to do so unless his wounds are so severe that he is incapable of carrying them. The soldier should be taught that it is a point of honour to carry his arms as long as he possibly can. Lightly wounded men who have disobeyed this order should be ordered back to bring their rifles and equipment with them.

Prisoners – It was noticed in many cases that escorts to prisoners were far too large. Escorts should never be larger than 15% of the number of prisoners.

Work by R.E. – It has been reported by R.E. Units that strong points which had been ordered to be consolidated were not always handed over on the relief of battalions. The work on these was therefore not continuous. Good liaison between R.E. Units and the brigades to which they are affiliated will assist materially in the continuity of work on strong points as these will become known to the field companies irrespective of whether the strong points had been handed over as such to the relieving infantry units or not. Covering parties should always be provided for the R.E. when working in the front line or in places where the exact position of the enemy is unknown.

Clearance of Battlefield – Whenever possible, special troops will be told off to assist the regimental stretcher bearers and bearer divisions of field ambulances with the bringing in of wounded men and for the burial of dead. This, however, is not always possible and it is the duty of local commanders to do all they can in these respects.

Relief – (a) Troops must be able to relieve those in the front line over the open (by night). Carefully marked out overland routes are as important for this purpose as for carrying parties. (b) The liaison officer from the battalion at brigade headquarters should be utilised to guide the incoming battalion, with guides, sent back specially for the purpose to brigade H.Q. to help him.

H.Q. 19th Division   Lieutenant-Colonel
15th July 1916   General Staff

* nettoyage – French meaning to clean up, nettoyer – one who mops up

N.B. The above notes were discovered amongst the papers of Charles Lander.

Appendix II
Days spent in line or in brigade reserve

Summary of number of days spent in line or when battalion was in brigade reserve

District or Sector	Time Spent
La Boiselle	*3days*
Bazentin and Mametz	*3 days*
Bazentin 2nd	*3 days*
Messines, Spanbroekmollen	*6 days*
Thiepval, Zollern Road	*3 days*
Thiepval Regina Trench	*about 8 days*
Grandcourt	*2 days*
Messines, Bois Carré	*6 days*
Messines	*5 days*
Oosttaverne	*4 days*
Ravine Wood etc.	*10 days*
Shrewsbury Forest and Hill 60	*10 days*
Cambrai, Marciong	*about 24 days*
Messines and Kemmel	*10 days*
Dickebush and Ouderdom	*12 days*
Total	**about 109 days**

The casualties of the 10th Battalion R Wks R amounted to 49 officers and 824 men killed or died of wounds. The number wounded would probably be four times this number but I have no record.

Of the officer casualties 35 were killed while I was serving with the battalion overseas, shewing how little of the serious business I missed.

It is rather curious that only four officers were killed during the first twelve months of active service and one of these, Mr Parsent threw his life away by ignoring repeated warnings of a sniper's activity at a certain spot. The month of July 1916 on the Somme accounted for fourteen officers killed in the three distinct actions. The trench warfare in autumn of 1916 lost us two brilliant young officers through utter foolhardiness. The three weeks on the Ancre culminating in the attack on Grandcourt 18/11/16 lost us five officers killed.

The most extraordinary year was 1917 and to March 1918 through fifteen months, including attack at Messines and 3rd battle of Ypres we only lost three officers killed; two of them, Mr Bostock and Mr Brazier, were killed by the same shell while in assembly positions before attack 20/9/17. From March 21st 1918 until the armistice our losses were very severe, sixteen officers killed in less than eight months.

Appendix III
Officer and R.S.M. casualties

Officer and R.S.M. casualties recorded by Charles Lander

- 1915 -

9/10/15   2nd-Lt Pinsent, Richard Parker. Aged 22, son of Hume C and Ellen F Pinsent of 8, Chelsea Court, Chelsea, London. Bullet to the head. Buried – Le Touret Military Cemetery, Richebourg-L'Avoue.

20/12/15   Lt Whitworth, E.S. Aged 24, son of Andrew Ernest and Annie Whitworth of Birmingham, husband of Winifred Lilian Whitworth of 24, Ivor Road, Sparkhill, Birmingham. Buried – St Vaast Post Military Cemetery, Richebourg-L'Avoue.

- 1916 -

7/1/16   Lt Ward, Charles Sandford. Aged 21, son of Herbert and Sarita Ward of Rolleboise, Seine-et-Oise, France. Memorial – Loos.

25/3/16   Lt Carty, William George. Aged 25, son of William James and Lucy Carty of 8, Guy's Cliffe Terrace, Warwick. Buried – Rue Du Bacquerot No. 1 Military Cemetery, Laventie.

2/07/16   2nd-Lt Williamson, Cyril George. Age 22, son of Sarah and the late Arthur Williamson of "Newlyn" Selly Park Road, Birmingham. Memorial – Thiepval.

3/7/16   2nd-Lt Rogers, Esmond Hallewell. Aged 25, son of Sir Hallewell Rogers, Kt., D.L., Honorary Colonel 68th Brigade. (T) R.F.A. and Lady Rogers, Greville Lodge, Edgbaston, Birmingham. Memorial – Thiepval.

3/7/16   Capt. Lynn Shaw Henry (acting Major). Aged 44, son of John Henry and Katherine Shaw of Kings Lynn, husband of Grace E Lynn Shaw of 2, Pakenham Road, Edgbaston, Birmingham. Buried – Bapaume Post Military Cemetery, Albert.

3/7/16   Capt. Heard, Geoffrey Richard. (Dr R.A.M.C.) – Aged 30, son of Richard William and the late Annie Louisa Heard of 7, Osbourne Villas, Devonport. Buried – Bapaume Post Military Cemetery, Albert.

4/7/16   Capt. Jones, Charles Edward Coursolles. Sent up the line as reinforcement on July 3rd. Memorial – Thiepval.

22/7/16   2nd-Lt Hewett, Stephen Henry Phillip. Aged 23, son of John and Mary Hewett of Exeter. Educated at Downside School and Balliol College. Memorial – Thiepval.

23/7/16   2nd-Lt Rainbow, Albert Edward – Aged 24, son of Charles and Harriet Rainbow of 5 Farley Street, Leamington Spa. Memorial – Thiepval.

23/7/16   2nd-Lt Clarke, George Edward. Memorial – Thiepval.

24/7/16   Maj. Henderson, Albert N (act Lt-Col.). Memorial – Thiepval.

24/7/16   2nd-Lt Marston, Felix. Aged 20, son of Mr H.W. Marston of 38, Kingswood Road, Moseley, Birmingham. Buried – St Pierre Cemetery, Amiens.

30/7/16   Capt. Bird, George Brown (M.C. and Bar). Aged 31, son of George and Emma Bird. Memorial Thiepval.

30/7/16   2nd-Lt Hart, Richard George. Aged 24, son of the late Frank Eden Hart and Amy Hart, brother of H. Wyatt Hart, of 205, Uchi Street, North Kana, Northern Rhodesia, a Rhodes Scholar. Buried – London Cemetery and Extension, Longueval.

30/7/16   2nd-Lt Pearson, Stanley Osborne. Memorial – Thiepval.

30/7/16   2nd-Lt Poole, John Richard. Aged 28, husband of Grace Elizabeth Poole of 13, Wattville Road, Handsworth, Birmingham. Memorial – Thiepval.

27/8/16   Lt Briscoe, Edward Villiers (act capt. and adj.). Aged 22, son of
           Maj. Edward William (late R.A.) and Helen Mary Briscoe of
           45, Longport Street, Canterbury, was serving as Adj. of 10th
           Battalion at the time of his death. Memorial – Menin Gate,
           Ypres.

15/9/16   2nd-Lt Woodbridge, Stephen Antony Ruston. Buried – South
           Ealing Cemetery.

18/11/16   2nd-Lt Smart, Eric Douglas. Aged 24, son of Mr and Mrs
           W.H. Smart of The Grange, Tanworth-in-Arden, Warwickshire.
           Memorial – Thiepval.

18/11/16   2nd-Lt Burley, Charles Frederick. Aged 18, son of C.A. Burley
           of 44, Hazelbury Crescent, Luton, Beds. and the late Richard
           Burley. Memorial – Thiepval.

18/11/16   2nd-Lt Gott, Albert Ernest (ass, adj.). Son of John Gott
           of Chateau les Frevaux, Malaunay, Seine Inferurie, France.
           Memorial – Thiepval.

18/11/16   2nd-Lt Needham, Pascall. (M.C.) – Memorial – Thiepval.

18/11/16   2nd-Lt Nutting, Ernest Ralph. Aged 37, son of the late William
           and Ellen Nutting. Memorial – Thiepval.

- 1917 -

8/6/17   2nd-Lt Cooper, Richard. Aged 27, husband of Mrs. A.M.
           Cooper of 1, Elm Road, Gillingham, Kent. Memorial – Menin
           Gate, Ypres.

20/9/17   2nd-Lt Bostock, Clifford. Aged 27, son of John and Emily
           Bostock of 10, St. Werburgh's Road, Chorlton-cum-Hardy,
           Manchester. M.Sc. Tech (Vic). Memorial – Tyne Cot.

20/9/17   2nd-Lt Brazier, Albert Edward. Aged 28, son of Albert and
           Emma Jane Brazier of The Shrubbery, Bromsgrove, husband of
           Edith Brazier of Rock Hill, Bromsgrove, Worcs. Memorial
           – Tyne Cot.

20/09/17   R.S.M. Pratt, Edward Joseph. Resident of Foleshill, Coventry.
           D.O.W. to the side. Buried – Bus House Cemetery near Ypres.

- 1918 -

23/3/18   2nd-Lt Burningham, Ralph Horace (Transport). Aged 32,
           husband of Mary E. Handley Burningham of High Leigh,
           Mycenae Road, Westcombe Park, Blackheath, London.
           Memorial – Arras.

23/3/18   2nd-Lt Morrall, John Bernard. Aged 39, son of Edward and
           Mary Morrall. Educated at Downside College. Memorial
           – Arras.

23/3/18   2nd-Lt Wilson, Edwin Thomas. Memorial – Arras.

10/4/18   Lt Jones, William Edgar. Aged 28, son of the late Rev. Thomas
           Jones of West Hill, Putney, London, husband of Lily Margaret
           Jones of "Glaslyn", Avenue Road, Abergavenny, Mon.
           Memorial – Tyne Cot.

11/4/18   2nd-Lt Pearson, John. Aged 25, son of John and Mary Pearson
           of 146, Ash Road, Saltley, Birmingham. Buried – Llissenthoek
           Military Cemetery.

15/4/18   2nd-Lt Wright, Victor Albert. Aged 28, son of Albert Henry
           and Catherine Wright of 25, Grange Road, Small Heath,
           Birmingham. Memorial – Tyne Cot.

26/4/18   2nd-Lt O'Neill, Douglas Quirk. Aged 27, son of Mr J. O'Neill
           of Lahore, India. Buried – Grootebeek British Cemetery.

5/5/18 Capt. Martineau, Clement (P.O.W. 10/4/18). Aged 21, son of Geoffrey Arthur and Jessie Clementina Martineau of Touchwood Hall, Solihull, Birmingham. Buried – Kortrijk (St Jan) Communal Cemetery.

10/5/18 2nd-Lt Richards, Ewart Wilfred (wounded 8/5/18). Aged 27, son of Mr and Mrs. S.S. Richards of "Glenhurst", 25, Nicholls Street, West Bromwich, Staffs. Buried – Arneke British Cemetery.

14/8/18 Capt. Coldicott, Arden Cotterell. (M.C.) – Aged 21, son of Arthur Cotterrell Coldicott and Annie Coldicott of Beaudesert, Henley in Arden, Birmingham. (See Service Record of King Edward's School, Birmingham 1920 page 31). Buried – Cologne Southern Cemetery.

21/9/18 Capt. Westwood, A.H. (attached from 6th Northants). Buried – Peronne Communal Cemetery Extension.

25/9/18 2nd-Lt Beaufoy, Clive Marston. Aged 21, son of Samuel M and Jane Alice Beaufoy of "The Beeches", Stratford Road, Shirley, Birmingham. Buried – Vielle-Chapelle New Military Cemetery.

20/10/18 Capt. Hewett, H.A. Buried – Cambrai East Military Cemetery.

8/11/18 2nd-Lt Cleave, Norman. Aged 21, son of Mr and Mrs Walter Cleave of The Bracken, Somerville Road, Sutton Coldfield, Birmingham. Buried – Malplaquet Communal Cemetery.

8/11/18 Capt. Stehn, Arthur Edward (twice mentioned in Despatches). Aged 24, son of George and Helenora Stehn (nee Heron-Maxwell), of Warrington, Seaford, Sussex. Buried – Malplaquet Communal Cemetery.

8/11/18 2/Lt Hyde, William Frederick. Aged 30, son of Joseph and Lydia Eliza Hyde, husband of Winifred Maude Hyde of 256, Aston Lane, Handsworth, Birmingham. Buried – Malplaquet Communal Cemetery.

10/11/18   Lt. Potter, Edward. Aged 32, son of Henry Potter of Sidcup, Kent, and the late Mary Ann Potter of 10, St. James' Terrace, Grimsby. Buried – St. Sever Cemetery Extension, Rouen.

13/11/18   2nd-Lt Wilson, Fred (died of wounds). Aged 27, son of Tom and Agnes Wilson of Ellerby, Yorks., husband of Winifred May Wilson of 100, Wills Street, Lozells, Birmingham. Buried – Mont Houn Military Cemetery, Le Treport.

25/11/18   Capt. Gribble, Julian Royds (V.C.) (P.O.W. 23/3/18). Aged 21, son of George James Gribble and Norah Gribble (née Royds) of Kingston Russell House, Dorset. Buried – Niederzwehren Cemetery.

Citation – An extract from "The London Gazette" No. 30770 dated 25th June 1918 records the following;

"For most conspicuous bravery and devotion to duty Capt. Gribble was in command of the right company of the battalion when the enemy attacked, and his orders were to 'hold on to the last'. His company was eventually entirely isolated, though he could easily have withdrawn them at one period when the rest of the battalion on his left were driven back to a secondary position. His right flank was 'in the air', owing to the withdrawal of all troops of a neighbouring division. By means of a runner to the company on his left rear he intimated his determination to hold on until other orders were received from battalion headquarters – and this he inspired his command to accomplish. His company was eventually surrounded by the enemy at close range, and he was seen fighting to the last. His subsequent fate is unknown. By his splendid example of grit, Capt. Gribble was materially instrumental in preventing for some hours the enemy obtaining a complete mastery of the crest of ridge, and by his magnificent self-sacrifice he enabled the remainder of his own brigade to be withdrawn, as well as another garrison and three batteries of field artillery".

- 1919 -

11/3/19   2nd-Lt Pegg, William John. Aged 28, son of D.W. and Ellen
           Pegg of Overstrand. Wounded 18/3/18. Buried – Overstrand
           (St Martin) Churchyard.

16/5/19   Capt. Hardy, Smith Arnold. Aged 38, son of Mr. and Mrs. R.
           Hardy Smith of Lewisham, London. Buried – Mikra British
           Cemetery, Kalamaria.

Sources: Commonwealth War Graves Commission
              Soldiers Died
              Battalion War Diary

Glossary

AAA	Full point using military signals (messages)
A.D.S.	Advanced Dressing Station
A.S.C.	Army Service Corps
Adj.	Adjutant (rank)
Base-wallah	From Anglo-Indian. Soldier employed behind the lines away from the front line
Beek	Flemish for brook
Black Line	Objective point within a military operation
Blue on Blue	Inadvertent firing on one's own or friendly troops
Bn	Battalion
Brig. Gen.	Brigadier General (rank)
C.C.S.	Casualty Clearing Station
C.B.	Confined to Barracks
C.O.	Commanding Officer
C.Q.M.S.	Company Quartermaster Master Sergeant
C.S.M.	Company Sergeant Major
Capt.	Captain (rank)
Catting	Vomitting
C.M.G.	Companion of the Order of St. Michael & St. George
Col	Colonel (rank)
Coy	Company
Cpl	Corporal
C.R.E.	Corps of Royal Engineers / Commander of Royal Engineers
D.C.M.	Distinguished Conduct Medal
D.P.S.	Delayed Primary Suture
D.S.O.	Distinguished Service Order
D.O.W.	Died of Wounds

Estaminet	Small cafe serving coffee, beer, wine & the most popular of all French dishes of the time - egg & chips
F.S.	Field Service
Gen.	General (rank)
G.O.C.	General Officer Commanding
Green Line	Objective point within a military operation
H.E.	High Explosive
H.Q.	Headquarters
I.B.D.	Infantry Base Depot
L.N.W.R.	London & North Western Railway
Lt	Lieutenant
Lt-Col	Lieutenant Colonel (rank)
M.C.	Military Cross
M.G.	Machine Gun
M.G.O.	Master-General of the Ordnance
M.O.	Medical Officer
M.P.	Military Policeman
Maj.	Major
Minenwerfer	German short range mortar
N.C.O.	Non-commissioned Officer
O.C.	Officer Commanding / Officer Cadet
O.T.C.	Officers Training Corps
P.B.I.	Poor Bloody Infantry
P.O.W.	Prisoner of War
P.T.	Physical Training
Pip-Squeak	German high explosive high velocity field gun shell
Pte	Private (rank)
Q.M.	Quartermaster
Qui Vive	Alert
R.A.M.C.	Royal Army Medical Corps
R.A.O.C.	Royal Army Ordnance Corps
R.C.	Roman Catholic
R.O.D.	Rail Ordnance Depot / Royal Ordnance Depot
R.E.	Royal Engineers
R.F.C.	Royal Flying Corps
R.P.	Regimental Police

R.S.M.	Regimental Sergeant Major
R.T.O.	Railway Transport Officer
R. Wks R	Royal Warwickshire Regment (R Wks Regt)
S.A.A.	Small Arms Ammunition
S.B.	Stretcher Bearer
Sgt	Sergeant (rank)
S.J.	Society of Jesus
S.O.S.	Emergency distress call
Stokes	Gun/Mortar - trench mortar invented by British engineer Wilfrid Stokes in 1915
Sub	Sub Altern (rank). Young junior officer
V.C.	Victoria Cross
Verey/Very	Aerial flares used to watch enemy activity at night or to illuminate no man's land.
Whizz-bang	A field gun shrapnel shell fired at close range
W.O.	War Office
Y.M.C.A.	Young Men's Christian Association

List of Subscribers

Thanks go to the following and the members of The Guild Of Battlefield Guides whose support enabled this work to be published.

Mark Bentley

Michael Booker

Tony Coutts-Britton

John Cotterill

Steven Dieter

Simon French

Ryan Gearing

Rob Gerrard FRGS

Dudley Giles

Clive Harris

Michael Harrison

Pete Hawtin

Brett Hayward

Alison Hine

Dave Holmes

Prof. Richard Holmes CBE

Jo Hook

Miriam Llewellyn

Revd Les Mather

Paul Naish, Major (retired)

Christopher Preston

Andrew Riddoch

Tony Smith

Iain Standen

Piers Storie-Pugh OBE

Gary D Waer

Dennis Weatherall

Simon Worrall

Jon Wort

For more information on The Guild of Battlefield Guides, please visit www.gbg-international.com

Index